Ma：　　̣ ̣ was born in the old West Riding of Yorkshire, just　　 the outbreak of the Second World War. He started collec　 ̣ antiques at an early age, hoarding his treasures in a disuse　 ̣n house, known ever after as the 'junk hut'.

Aft　 National Service and a brief period working for an engin　 ̣ng company, Max and his family heard the call of the Y　̣shire Dales, where they bought a cottage, hung out their s　　 – Bullpen Antiques – and made a happy living for many 　 ̣rs.

Ma：　 ̣d his family now live in Leyburn, North Yorkshire, with t　 ̣ dogs, two ponies, a goat named Elspeth and an ever-fl　 ̣uating population of hens, ducks and pigeons. His only r　 ̣et is that he no longer has the contents of his tr　 ̣ ̣　 'junk hut'.

Praise for the *Tales from the Dales* series

'A happy, satisfying and very funny book' James Herriot

'Cunningly observed, shrewd, wicked and wittily entertaining' *Daily Mail*

'A cross between *All Creatures Great and Small* and *Lovejoy* . . . entertaining and humorous' *Yorkshire Post*

TALES FROM THE DALES

A Countryman's Lot

MAX HARDCASTLE

SPHERE

First published in Great Britain in 1990 by the Penguin Group
First published in paperback in 1992 by Warner Books
This paperback edition published in 2011 by Sphere

A CIP catalogue for this book
is available from the British Library.

ISBN 978-0-7515-4419-0

Typeset in Baskerville by M Rules
Printed and bound in Great Britain by
Clays Ltd, St Ives plc

Sphere
An imprint of
Little, Brown Book Group
100 Victoria Embankment
London EC4Y 0DY

An Hachette UK Company
www.hachette.co.uk

www.littlebrown.co.uk

To my wife Sandra

Chapter 1

'There's your Arthur-type place.' Colin slapped the folded newspaper on to the counter in front of me and dropped on to a chair. 'Any chance of a coffee, love?' he said, grinning up at Vicky, who dutifully disappeared up the stairs to the kitchen.

Colin was between girlfriends and, although it was almost lunchtime, it was obvious he had not been out of bed for long.

I leaned over the newspaper and read the advertisement he'd ringed in red crayon. 'Lot 1, comprising twenty acres of sound . . .'

'No! No!' interjected Colin, 'lot 3, the farmhouse.' The ill-defined photograph showed a long low farmhouse with attached barn, a typical Yorkshire dales steading. I read on silently: 'Freehold farmhouse with outbuildings, orchard and garth, in all totalling three acres. The house, in need of some renovation, commands a . . .'

I read the advertisement half a dozen times before Vicky shouldered the door open and laid a tray of coffee and biscuits on a table.

'Well, what do you think?' I said, turning the newspaper towards her.

She read it in silence, nodding her head slightly at the end of each sentence. 'That's the bit that worries me.' She scored a thin line with her fingernail under 'in need of some renovation'. 'And where exactly is it? It says "North Yorkshire, unspoilt village", but I've never heard of Ramsthwaite.'

Colin rubbed the rim of the coffee cup across his lower lip thoughtfully. 'Ah, yes, I've been through it a few times. Dead-alive hole, just a shop and a pub.' He lifted his feet on to a chair opposite and clacked his shoes together. 'Personally, I don't know why you want to leave this place.'

To Colin, the little terraced shop with its flat above was paradise: in a busy thoroughfare, with a pub next door and a fish and chip shop opposite, a kitchen to warm his can of beans in and a secluded rear bedroom where he could entertain his latest girlfriend; it had everything he needed – except that he didn't live here. The shoes clicked together again.

'You'll sell this easy enough, especially with the smashing flat.'

Neither Vicky nor I agreed with him on that point. With two children, Peter aged nine and Sally aged seven, two spaniels and no storage to speak of, the tiny flat was crammed to overflowing.

Three years before, the company I had worked for since leaving college had been taken over and, after six months of assurances, I had been called to head office. After a brief interview I had walked out into the corridor in a daze, a cheque in my hand and no job.

Months of letter writing and interviews had followed, each

2

rejection bringing a period of self-doubt. Vicky had watched sympathetically until she had realized, with that down-to-earth practicality women have, that something had to be done.

She had taken the latest nicely worded rejection letter from my hand, screwed it into a ball and thrown it into the fire. 'Let's sell the house and open that antique shop we've always dreamed of – but we must do it *now*, before the redundancy money is gone.'

We both had a love of antiques and, since the early years of our marriage, had collected and dealt in them for fun. In fact, we felt that our knowledge and skills were equal to those of many a dealer who was making a good living.

Within two months we had sold our comfortable house in Birmingham, with the neat lawns and California-style kitchen, moved into the little terraced shop and opened our doors to the antique-hungry residents of south Leeds.

Colin had been our very first customer. He'd breezed into the shop on our first morning open, bought the two best pieces of silver in the place, left a grubby business card and breezed out with a cheery, 'See you next week.'

Vicky had looked at me and shrugged her shoulders. 'Seems a bit of a character.'

He started to call upon us regularly, and his battered van pulling up in front of the shop became the signal for a coffee break. His jokey manner camouflaged a very astute mind. He had a thorough knowledge of period silver and would inter-sperse periods of extreme idleness with weeks of very hard work, travelling throughout the north of England buying and selling. His contacts were wide and diverse and it was when I had bought a load of seasoned English oak beams from a woodyard sale that he had put me in touch with Arthur.

3

Selling to Arthur did not prove to be an easy task, especially over the telephone. He punctuated my description of the oak with non-committal 'aye's, and when I finished there followed a long awkward silence, then, 'You say it's not shaked?'

'No, it's not shaked.'

'You say it's well seasoned?'

'It's well seasoned.'

'You say there's no whip in it?'

'There's no whip in it.'

Another even longer silence followed. I tried a tentative 'hello' or two, thinking we'd been cut off, and I was just going to put down the receiver when Arthur's voice came over loud and clear, 'If you'll deliver it for that price, I'll have it.'

The following Sunday we loaded the van and, throwing a mattress on top of the timber for the children and dogs to sit on, set off north for the Yorkshire dales, to see for the first time the little smallholding which was to sow the seeds of discontent with our way of life and send us searching for our own 'Arthur-type place'.

Arthur Fothergill was a retired joiner who faked eighteenth-century refectory tables. They were passed into the trade through a London dealer who constantly pestered Arthur to increase his output, but Arthur was unmovable: 'I make two tables a year, and that's it.'

Some years previously, he had bought two lorryloads of oak planking which had come from the stables of a stately home. The oak had been fumed with ammonia from the horse drop-pings and when finished it came up a glorious dark brown. Arthur had adequate oak for the plank tops and stretchers, but the legs presented him with a problem. He needed eight-inch-square oak, of turnable quality, to work his variations on the design of each set of legs; vase, cannon barrel, cup-and-cover, Arthur excelled at them all. The beams we had taken him that Sunday afternoon enabled the annual production to continue for a good few years.

Arthur was a consummate craftsman; every mortice and tenon was hand cut, every dowel the product of a drawknife. He had studied his subject carefully, long hours spent in museums and stately homes in diligent study enabling him to produce a table which fooled all but the really expert. Not for him the smooth, even, simulated wear of lesser hands; he knew how a 250-year-old table should look. The underside of the top planks were put through his frame-saw and worked on a rocking table to produce the irregular cuts expected from pit sawing. The legs and stretchers were distressed with chain flails, and a little acid produced the convincing rot found at the base of every table leg which has spent decades on a damp stone-flagged floor.

Each table spent six months in Arthur's workshop and then six months in his comfortable farmhouse kitchen, where the finishing touches were added. The edge of the underside was rubbed with old mutton fat to simulate the caress of a thousand greasy fingers and the top, after being treated with dyed linseed oil, was beeswaxed daily. Black lead was applied around the joints to fake the build-up of age-hardened polish. When Arthur had finished a table, it delighted the eye.

His hobby was breeding the big woolly Wensleydale sheep. Slow to mature and prone to single lambing, they have been ousted from the dales flocks by the hardy Swaledale, but in Arthur's eyes they could do no wrong.

Some years before, Arthur's wife had had a wish to spin and knit up some of the superb wool of the Wensleydales, and

Arthur dutifully made her a Hebridean-type spinning wheel. Following his natural inclination he produced a perfect copy, aged and patinated. When his only daughter was married the purse was a little thin, so the spinning wheel was dispatched to the auction room. As the hammer fell at an astonishing price, Arthur muttered a comment to the effect that the buyer was not only ill-advised but illegitimate into the bargain. The wheel is now the centrepiece of a little cottage tableau in a highly respected museum.

Colin got up slowly and stretched. It was one of his idle periods. He indicated that I could keep the newspaper and made for the door. 'Well, if you sell this place you must be bloody crackers.'

Vicky picked up the newspaper and tapped her chin with it. 'I'll give them a ring and get some particulars.'

I looked out across the rain-swept road. The bank's windows were already filled with pale yellow light and in the fish and chip shop a young girl scraped the last of the Christmas decorations from behind the glass door. 'Why not? Can't do any harm.'

Neither Vicky nor I are town dwellers by nature. We were both born and brought up in rural areas, and as I had moved around the country for my firm we had always managed to find a house which was at least near open country. Although, as Colin put it, 'we had everything', we still hankered after a life in the country.

We did not do a lot of trade with Arthur. He bought a little scrap wood from us every now and then and did us the odd repair; over a period of a year we would see him perhaps two or three times. The children revelled in these visits, playing in the stream and running wild over the moor with the dogs. We envied Arthur's quality of life, his cosy farmhouse with its magnificent views, his barns and garth.

Living as we did over our tiny shop, we were desperately cramped. Our back-up stock overflowed into the bedrooms; when we went to bed we picked our way across a floor littered with jampans, copper kettles, brass candlesticks and the odd warming pan. The landing was lined with hall-stands and washstands, and cardboard boxes full of bric-a-brac stood on the stairs.

On warm summer evenings we used to sit in the little stone-flagged yard and dream of what we had come to call our 'Arthur-type place'. If only we could find a place like that: a proper house with a big garden, apple trees, a small garth and masses and masses of storage room: a huge barn we could fill with pine, instead of stacking it ten feet high in the tiny yard.

The boundaries of our fantasy world were elastic, so when Vicky thought of any new feature we would add it to our dream. 'I want a stream, a stream we can hear as we lie in bed,' so a tinkling stream was pencilled into our castle in the dales. The dogs never tired of the faeces-strewn park, but the children fed on our fantasies and became increasingly disenchanted with our town life.

In the later years of Queen Victoria's reign, the area we lived in had been prosperous. Woollen mills and engineering factories had supplied the needs of an empire and the captains of industry, imbued with civic pride, had invested their profits in stone. The town – for in those days it had been separate from the city of Leeds – had boasted wide streets of blue setts, lined with imposing granite buildings. Balconets and Gothic turrets

7

abounded. Every blue slate roof was pierced by ornate dormers before it climbed to its terracotta-crested peak. When these worthy men had seen to the sewers and laid out a park, they sent for the foundry catalogues and sprinkled the streets with acanthus-wreathed gas lamps. The two Jubilees of Victoria brought the horse trough and cast-iron bandstand.

Now the setts are tarmacked over, the streets are efficiently lit with sodium from concrete stalks and the buildings rise from a froth of neon and perspex. It is a friendly area; complete strangers will stick their head through the door. 'By, I like that chest o' drawers. If I win the pools . . .'

Some mornings I would have a few words with the landlord in the pub next door. We could not see each other. I would hear him stacking his empty crates in the yard and stand at the back door in slippered feet, to shout up at the wall, 'Have a good night, Harry?'

'No, a few tight buggers in.'

He never had a good night, but there is a new car in the garage and a son away at public school.

We had no views from the flat. The rear windows looked over the yard on to the red brick wall of a four-storey woollen mill, its hammered glass windows thick with grime and its gutters bowed and filled with weed. At the front, across the High Street, a Victorian Gothic bank blocked out the afternoon sunlight, rising like the superstructure of a battleship from the row of terraced shops. We knew every square inch of its sooty ash-tarred stones.

We found Ramsthwaite on the map – a tiny dot high on the contours between the River Swale and the River Ure. When the auctioneer's details arrived, complete with its little map outlining the property in red, we could not wait to go and see it.

Colin agreed to man the shop for us, and the children wore us down with a night of, 'It's not fair', and, 'Why can't we go?', until we agreed to let them miss school and come with us.

Bullpen Farm stood at the top of the village green, long and low under its stone-flagged roof. Built in the last quarter of the eighteenth century, it had good dressed-stone quoins and deep headers to its doors and windows. The roof sagged badly and bright green cushion moss grew between its ridge stones. The windows, horizontal sliding Yorkshire lights, were rotten to the touch, but the massive oak-planked door, cramped and hugged by hand-wrought hinges that stretched across its full width, was as sound as a bell. There were no pots on the chimney stacks but slates set tent fashion, to turn the worst of the rain.

The outbuildings were in better shape than the house, which had not been lived in for five years. An eight-stall cow byre was set against the west wall of the house and across the puddled yard stood a two-storey building with an outside staircase – the apple house. In the orchard, aged fruit trees, their gnarled limbs white with bird lime, rose from a sea of brown grass and briar. Beyond the orchard a two-acre garth stretched like a green thumb up the lower slope of the fell. The eastern boundary was formed by a clear stream, which busied itself between high banks and over a bright pebbled bottom until the culvert under the road swallowed it noisily. Alongside the stream stood a small Dutch barn; two poultry arks, their boards bleached and sprung, were half hidden in the stalky grass.

Vicky fetched the key from the farm next door and we trampled the briar and elder to get in. All the rooms, with the exception of the dairy, had the same striped wallpaper and every door and skirting board was painted the same chocolate brown. A huge Yorkist range filled one wall of the kitchen. Its knobs and dampers, once polished and handled to shiny perfection, now stood out red and pimply with rust against the black ironwork.

We stood at the bedroom window and watched the children race up and down the apple house steps, until they tired and pushed open the door of the two-seater earth closet to grin at the smooth round holes.

I held Vicky's hand for a full five minutes before I blurted out, 'Shall we have a crack?'

She smiled back at me. 'Colin keeps saying we're crackers, why not?'

All the way home we talked of nothing but the farm and how it fitted in with our dream. The children, as children do, saw no problems and when we got back to the shop they shook a sleepy Colin awake. 'We've found our farm,' they chanted.

We put our shop on the market the following day. There followed three frantic weeks of organizing. Bridging loans, surveyor's reports, arguing with the estate agent and pleading with the bank manager, and showing a trickle of prospective buyers over the shop and flat. In the evenings we littered the kitchen table with plans, sketches and estimates, and when we sank into our beds we lay awake pondering the enormity of the step we were taking. Many nights we lay in the dark, each knowing what the other was thinking. We whispered into the pillows, 'It'll be great for the children.' 'We'll make a go of it.' 'We're a good team, kid – we'll do it.' And so we bolstered each other's confidence and kept the fears at bay, until sleep laid its kind hand on us.

*

The day of the auction in Ramsthwaite arrived. We had had a lot of interest in our shop but as yet had not found a firm buyer. The planning authorities had been quite helpful. There was a lot of derelict and semi-derelict property in the dale and anyone wishing to make it their home and earn a living from it got a sympathetic hearing. They could see no objections to our plans, provided we stayed within certain guidelines.

The auction attracted a large crowd. There were several lots of good grazing to come under the hammer that day and the local farmers, fortified with a glass or two, climbed the stairs to the long room over The Ship, the pub on the other side of the village green, and arrayed themselves for battle. By the time we had settled the children in the van with pop and crisps there was standing room only. We edged our way through the noisy crowd to the back of the smoke-filled room.

Lots 1 and 2 must have fetched record prices for grazing land in the dale, for the quiet of the bidding gave way to a hubbub of noise each time the hammer fell.

As the auctioneer announced, 'Lot 3, Bullpen Farm,' our hearts beat wildly, we held hands and pressed our shoulders together. I started the bidding tentatively, and the auctioneer dutifully took bids 'off the wall' until the reserve was reached, then, bringing his hammer down with a cursory nod, he sent his clerk scurrying down the aisle to escort us to the table. I signed the agreement and handed over a cheque for ten per cent of the hammer price.

With sweaty palms and pounding hearts we ran up the village green to tell the children, 'Bullpen Farm is ours.'

I hooked my arms under the sagging gate and jerked it open. The children careered around the yard, leaping the brown puddles. 'It's ours! It's ours!'

Hand in hand, Vicky and I climbed to the top of the garth. We sat down and smiled at each other. 'Happy?' I asked her. She leaned her forehead against mine; her gentle blue eyes shone with excitement. 'We must be crackers,' she whispered. I put my arms around her and we fell sideways, rolling for three full turns through the soaking February grass.

We lay laughing up at the grey sky, until a red moon of a face appeared over the wall. Vicky tapped my chest. 'It's the man I got the key from.'

I scrambled to my feet and pulled Vicky up. We stood there, feeling embarrassed, while the moon face stared at us in silence. Several seconds passed before it returned my greeting with a friendly nod, then disappeared.

Chapter 2

The surveyor's report had made pretty depressing reading. The house needed major repairs but at least it was basically sound. During the six weeks between the auction and the completion date, Vicky and I made several visits to Ramsthwaite. We spent the mornings going over the house and byre, measuring and prodding, and making endless lists which lay before us on the table in The Ship, the village pub, at lunchtime.

'Going to be an antique shop, then.' The owner of the red moon face which had peered at us over the garth wall brought his pint and pulled a stool up to our table. 'I'm Ted, I live next door.'

We introduced ourselves and shook the big red hand. The villagers had obviously seen our planning application. We had been wondering how they would react to an antique shop in the village, so I tried to pull him out on the subject. 'Do you think we'll make a fortune?'

He grinned at us for several seconds, then nodded towards the bar. 'He's the only bugger as makes a fortune in this village.'

The landlord ignored him. His head resting on his hands, he stared steadily into the fire.

Ted took a long pull at his beer. 'They're long winters up here. I suppose you know your business.' The landlord blew down his nose. 'They're long winters up here.'

I kept Ted's glass filled and he warmed to his task of instructing us about the village, until the landlord called time. Screwing on his cap he insisted on shaking hands with us again.

'Well, I hope the countryman's lot suits you. Anyway, it'll be nice to see t'owd house lived in again.'

We still had not sold our Leeds shop and the interest on the bridging loan was worrying us. The planning application had gone through without a hitch, so it was becoming obvious that we would have to concentrate on the byre conversion and open for business in the dale as soon as we could, preferably before Easter. With great trepidation, therefore, we arranged a date for our furniture and stock to go into storage, and took ourselves off in search of a static caravan.

Neither of us relished the idea. Summers spent caravanning with the children in the earlier years of our marriage had dampened any enthusiasm we might have had for caravan life. It had always rained. Endless games of Ludo and Snakes and Ladders had whiled away the afternoons, until boredom had made us reach for our wellingtons and brave the weather.

After a week of searching, we had found a twenty-six-foot Pemberton. Of uncertain vintage, it had been well maintained and its careful owners had lavished love and attention on its interior. Little crocheted mats were dotted here and there, and a fitted zinc tray crowded with house plants filled the bay window. Every cranny had a door or a shelf or a hook. Storage space, we were told, was the key. A place for everything and everything in its place. It made it heaven for the believer and bearable for the non-believer.

The caravan arrived on a low-slung articulated lorry, with the most unhelpful driver imaginable. He grunted an objection to every siting we proposed. Finally, we managed to get the caravan parallel to the cow byre, its chic bow window breasting the orchard fence. As soon as it was up on its jacks, I set to with pick and shovel and laid a plastic water pipe to it from the kitchen; running water we had to have. I rooted spars and posts from under the Dutch barn and cobbled together a rough lean-to. We needed all the covered space we could get. The lean-to proved to be a boon, we cooked in it, ate in it, and the dogs reluctantly slept in it.

We put the majority of our furniture and all of our stock into store and, on the last Sunday in March, moved into the caravan.

The following day, two reluctant children were dragged across the village green and, with many protests and a few tears from Sally, were enrolled at the village school. By the time Vicky had returned from that task I had demolished most of the cow byre partitions. Stripped to the waist, I swung the sledgehammer, crushing the larger lumps, while Vicky worked away with a garden rake pulling the rubble into the dung passage, tamping and levelling so as to leave it a good three inches below the level of the stalls.

The sound of the hammer blows brought next-door Ted into the byre. He looked sadly at the shattered concrete stalls. 'Ar wish you'd 'ave said. I could 'ave done wi' them boskins.'

By lunchtime, the partitions were out and the centre of the

floor ready for its new skim of concrete. All afternoon I barrowed aggregate from the back yard and fed the temperamental little mixer. It was time to fetch the children from school as I tamped and floated out the last of the mix.

We had intended going back after tea, to start scraping the walls, but as I lay on the bed tiredness welled over me and my arms ached from shovelling and swinging the heavy hammer, so we set the portable television in the middle of the houseplants and spent a guilty evening at rest.

Within the week, the walls and woodwork had been stripped and a new door led out on to the village green. The electrics were rudimentary: rust-pitted conduit ran up one wall and across the roof, feeding pendant lights and an old round pin socket which had served the little compressor for the milking unit. I had drawn the fuses and started to prise the old conduit from the roof, when half a bearded face appeared at the open window.

'Rewiring it, are you?' it asked.

'It's a bit antiquated,' I replied.

The face disappeared from the window, and Baz pushed open the door. 'I put that in, nineteen years ago.'

I looked down from the ladder, a twisted length of conduit in my free hand. I felt a little guilty. 'Well, it's lasted all right, but it's a bit rough for the shop.' I didn't want to offend him.

'Edgar didn't like electric. He was always frightened of cutting through a wire and killing hisself. That's why I put it in conduit. He used to switch the lights on and off with a stick, and he wouldn't change a bulb for 'owt. I used to come and change 'em for him.'

I'd heard them talk of Baz in the pub. He earned his living

16

walling and hedging, and was reputed to be able to turn his hand to anything. I reckoned that if the wiring had lasted nineteen years without actually killing the cautious Edgar, he must be quite competent. Gently I enquired whether or not he still did electrical work.

By nightfall, Baz had neat runs of wiring to three new lights and a double socket sat under each window. We flicked the lights on and off gleefully and tested each socket with the one-bar electric fire. Everything worked perfectly. Baz made off across to The Ship as we bundled the children into bed. We were content with the day's work.

'Who was that man?' asked Sally as I tucked her in. 'I didn't like him.'

'That's Baz,' I told her. 'I like him, he can do electric.'

Baz started to appear every evening. He rendered, plastered and painted, and I fell naturally into the role of his labourer. He was a fast and skilled worker, never stopping for the mugs of coffee Vicky brought into the byre, which grew cold on the window sill. I worried what to pay him. Every time I asked him what he wanted he would reply, 'Give us what you think.' The sum I came up with, plus the odd pint at The Ship, seemed highly acceptable.

Cramped though the caravan was, we soon developed a workable routine. I would get up first and, after putting the kettle on the gas ring, awaken the children. Peter and Sally would swing their legs out of their bunks and, with eiderdowns pulled tightly around them, tuck into cornflakes and milk, while Vicky and I had our first coffee of the day. After turning out the dogs I would light the gas ring in the lean-to and start our breakfast, as Vicky got the children ready for school. We always breakfasted well and leisurely, for we had long, hard days and were great believers in stoking the boilers.

For Vicky, never a lover of housework, the one redeeming feature of caravan dwelling was that it was easy to clean. I would leave her at this task every morning and, calling the dogs, take a walk around the village.

Viewed from the fell top, the village is surprisingly compact. There are six council houses on the old cricket field now and the incongruous red brick of the Martins's bungalow glares from its collar of cypresses, but in the main it is a happy, harmonious blend of stone and slate. Although outside the National Park, the planners keep a careful eye on the village. It is not pretty, but the villagers know what they have and guard it as jealously as any zealous bureaucrat. It is still a busy workaday community; it gives the feeling of a place where life has always been hard but worthwhile.

Although the oldest houses in the village are early seventeenth-century, there is evidence that the site was occupied in pre-Roman times. Flint and bronze implements have been turned up in the gardens and the surrounding fields, and on the southern slope of Altondale Fell there are several hut circles.

It must have been an ideal site for early man for, with his back to the craggy fell and an abundant supply of good water, it would have been an easily defensible place against any enemy advancing from the south across the Plain of York. The surrounding country has obviously been grain-growing land, for the fields on the lower slopes of the fell have been terraced and the mill is mentioned in the Domesday Book. The beck, which rises high on the fell and bisects the village, has never been known to dry up. A long dry spell will reduce it to a mere

18

trickle, but a quick snow melt turns it into a raging torrent flooding through our farmyard and out across the village green, rolling boulders before it bigger than a man's head.

In the past, the whole dale belonged to a powerful monastery which had grown wealthy from the backs of sheep, and sheep are still the mainstay of the local agricultural economy. There are two sizeable dairy herds in the village and the softer land to the east is feeling the plough for the first time in nearly seventy years, but the sheep are still supreme. Their fleeces pay the rent and their lambs put guineas in the pocket.

After the decline of the lead mines the Estate was the biggest employer for miles around; in its Edwardian heyday it stabled over a hundred horses and its gamekeepers paraded like a small army. With one or two notable exceptions, the owners of the Estate have always looked benevolently upon the village. Its retired servants still receive largess in the form of the odd brace of pheasant and a load of logs at Christmas. During the years of the Depression it set the local men to work building a huge wall, in this case along its northern boundary, thus enabling the stonemason, the labourer, the carter and the quarryman to feed their children and put a little money into the village economy. The present owner has a degree in agriculture and has worked hard to make the Estate economically viable. Large stands of hardwoods have been felled, the ornamental ponds filled in and the orangery bulldozed away. The garden statuary was crated and sent off to auction, and the guests at the shooting parties are now, for the most part, wealthy European businessmen who pay handsomely for the privilege.

Baz, who often acts as a beater, is amused by the economics of pheasant shooting. 'Up gets a guinea, bang goes a penny and down comes half-a-crown. What is it?' he asked the children.

They are mystified by guineas and half-crowns, and stare at him in silence.

While the lead mines were still productive, the village supported three pubs. Only The Ship has survived. The Fleece became Spion Kop House and The Miner's Arms is now the village shop. The older inhabitants still send their grandchildren off to, 'Fetch us a loaf of bread from the Miner's.'

'Miner's, Grandma?'

The bewildered look on the young face will bring a smile to the older one. 'It was a pub when I was your age,' they will explain.

The Ship was always the farmers' pub, while the other two belonged to the miners and smelters. There was great rivalry between the pubs, and the annual quoits and knur-and-spell matches between The Fleece and The Miner's always ended in a pitched battle on the common.

'That's why the grass there is so green,' explained Ted. 'For fifty years it wor fed on blood.'

The village is a stable community, with a proportion of retired people and only one holiday home. The bus service is minimal, but we are on a well-trodden tourist route so the shop and the pub flourish. The school is now down to twelve pupils; its high-windowed classrooms under their steep blue slate roof were built to hold five times that number. Miss Wells runs it single handed. With so few pupils she has dispensed with the formal classroom layout and the children sit round her in a semi-circle. We tell Peter and Sally how lucky they are to experience this real village school. They both adore Miss Wells and neither of them likes the idea of being bussed out of the dale to a cold, impersonal school.

Miss Wells is everything; she is the font of all knowledge. A thin, quite pretty woman with bright eyes and a ready smile, teaching is her life. Every evening we have the pearls of Miss Wells's wisdom relayed to us, and every weekend we tramp miles looking for new specimens for her nature table. Miss Wells has taught at the school for a quarter of a century; it has been her life. She keeps a scrapbook, neat pages carrying photographs of school events and newspaper clippings covering almost a hundred years. One past pupil has sat in the American Senate and another became a famous music-hall star, but the overwhelming majority have turned out of the wrought-iron gates to become miners, farm boys and servants. Miss Wells has had her successes. One brief note she cherishes and finds too precious to stick in the scrapbook is on Oxford University notepaper. It came from a shy, awkward boy whom she had instilled with a love of knowledge and guided to grammar school. It reads simply, 'I've made it, Miss Wells – God bless you.'

Ted went to this school. The headmaster, for there was a staff of three in those days, had his customary word with the fourteen-year-old boy on his last day at school.

'Well, Edward.' 'Edward' indeed! – after nine years of 'You, boy', or, 'Smithson'. 'You don't seem to have learned a great deal in your time with us.'

Ted had waited until the gate was safely between them. 'I'm not surprised, I've spent half the time in t'bloody corner wi' me back to thi.'

Next to the school stands the Methodist chapel. Small and neat, its iron railings, spear-topped, guard two daisy-flocked squares of grass. Services are held there every other Sunday, when the cars of the 'good folk', as Baz calls them, are parked the length of the green. Miss Wells's thin legs pump the harmonium and her ringless fingers flit over its yellowed keys. 'Come, ye thankful people, come.' They are thankful people; good, honest, decent, hard-working people.

Before the coming of the internal combustion engine the village prospered, having a spur of the railway no more than a mile from its southern boundary. Twice a day the horsedrawn floats, their churns rattling, clattered through the village to catch the milk trains. The carter had his depot at Ramsthwaite, and the brightly painted produce of the drop-forge and foundry rested there before creeping up the dale on his two-horse wagon. Milk and mutton, cheese and wool flooded out of the fertile dale and the products of Victorian engineering and ingenuity flowed in.

Baz remembered his father telling him that, when he was a boy, 'There wasn't a blade of grass on that village green. It was worn to mud with wagons and traps.'

The wheelwright, the blacksmith and the bootmaker had good years, during which spacious, proud new houses were built in the village. Prospect House and Jubilee House; no mock Tudor timbering or false mullions for them, they were built by confident people in an age of confidence.

The first casualty of twentieth-century economics was the bootmaker. The gentry bought their fine riding boots elsewhere and the influx of clogs and cheap factory-made boots soon took the bread from his mouth. The blacksmith and the wheelwright fared better. The railway, paradoxically, created a need for more horses, for goods and produce had to be brought to, and distributed from, every railhead and station. The smith had it best: not only were there more horses to be shod, but the new machinery which agriculture now demanded had crept up to the very dalehead, and it all had to be maintained. The wheelwright survived on repair work – the dales were harsh on the spoked wheel – but the occasional new coup cart still left his shop after the Second World War.

The mill ground corn until the 1930s. Now its Crossley gas engine stands silent; its fine green livery with its yellow lining has given way to rust and the flywheel is solid in the huge bearings.

The mill is derelict but the miller's house, ivy-clad and guarded by a rank of millstones, stands alongside it bright with care. Its paint is whiter than white, its gate swings well and its tiny garden is hoed and clipped, pruned and sprayed into perfection. Mr and Mrs Moorhouse do bed and breakfast. The happy guests climb the steep wood staircase to the second floor, marvelling at the size of the beams, and settle into the chintzy comfort of the bedrooms.

If the tourists like the village, they love the shop. The cracked concrete floor is swept and clean, and the ranks of bowed shelves are heavy with tins. A chocolate-brown counter is cluttered with sweet jars. Mrs Lewis bobs her grey head over them as her skinny arm works the bacon slicer. A pink hand cradles each slice as it falls from the machine and then turns it deftly on to the greaseproof paper.

The shop smells of bacon and meal, of paraffin and cheese. It is renowned for its cheese. The big muslin-covered cheeses sit on a broad scrubbed plank; they are tapped and sniffed at until Mr Lewis thinks they are 'right'. The tester is plunged into them, twisted and withdrawn. Its thin core of cheese is pressed between finger and thumb and tasted slicer. The decision is slow in coming, for a good cheese, like a good wine, does not burst on to the palate.

Mr Lewis lifts his eyes to the whitewashed ceiling. 'Fit for a king.'

A request for wellingtons or slippers sends dancing the cards of shoelaces and glues on the narrow door to the stairs. Mrs Lewis's footsteps creak over the yellowed ceiling in search of a nine or an eight. She shouts down the stairs, 'I've got a brown in an eight.'

The shop sells everything. There are rows of greetings cards for every occasion, old-fashioned cards, shiny roses and woodland scenes. Old Mr Hall, Mrs Lewis's father, sits at the back of the shop. He weighs out potatoes and dispenses the paraffin. Now hard of hearing, he cranes forward to catch the gossip – gnarled hands clenched over the heavy stick, his eyes bright and intent. Paraffin takes a long time. He pads down the stone-flagged passage to the lean-to. The can fills slowly for he never turns the tap fully on. He sits on a stool by the huge tank, listening to the dribble of the liquid. There are cans which are bad fillers and cans which are good fillers. He is not fond of his paraffin job – it takes him away from the warm shop and the gossip.

We use the shop as much as we can; what does it matter that the cans of peas are pence dearer than they are in Lalbeck? The smells, the atmosphere and the friendliness of the shop are priceless.

Because the village is equidistant from the two noble rivers, I'd asked Ted whether it was in Wensleydale or Swaledale. He'd replied by spitting into the beck which divides the village green and pointing at the little frothy ball as it bobbed away.

'That'll end up in the River Ure, so this must be Wensleydale.'

The western side of the beck is cut regularly and in spring is covered in daffodils, but the land to the east is almost as rough as the common. At the bottom of the green the beck was, in the past, tunnelled through two walls. Where they narrowed at the outlet, vertical slides were cut into the masonry to carry broad elm boards to dam the flow of water. This is the wash-fold, where the sheep were once brought to be washed prior to shearing. The washings were an event to look forward to in the village year. There were coppers to be earned by the young lads, and the jugs of ale brought out from the pubs ensured that many a villager went happily, if unsteadily, to his bed that night.

With the coming of the bus service in the early 1920s the beck was culverted under the road and the east wall of the wash-fold demolished so that the buses could negotiate the tight bend and take the moor road to the dalehead. No other event since the coming of the railway changed life in the dales as the buses did. It was now feasible for the dalesfolk to earn their living as far away as Richmond and Northallerton, and in due course the buses also brought the first incomers into the village.

Old Mr Hall delighted in telling us his tale about the buses. 'I started hoeing peas when the three o'clock pulled in. I'd done four rows of peas and started on the carrots when I noticed t'bus wor still in, so I went across to have a look. Both driver and t'clipper were fast asleep against the wash-fold. That bus were nearly an hour late into Lalbeck; crafty bugger let the spare wheel down and told 'em he'd had a puncture.'

Chapter 3

With the concrete floor of the byre sealed against dust and only the walls to emulsion and a carpet to lay to complete the shop, we felt confident in sending for our stock and chattels out of storage. They arrived three days later on a bright clear morning, just as I had finished laying the carpet, and soon the top half of the village green was covered with our possessions.

The antiques and our own furniture were completely mixed. Our careful planning and labelling of tea chests had gone completely awry. We would have to store our own furniture in the apple house, the only place which was dry and secure. The two-man team which came with the pantechnicon was anything but helpful. As in a lot of two-man teams, one half was bone idle and the other, resentful of his idleness, was determined to do no more than his share. Finally, with a little cajoling and a lot of bribery, we got all our belongings carefully stacked in the apple house. The antiques would lie on the green until Baz arrived and he and I could set them around the shop to Vicky's directions.

I sat on the garden wall, coffee mug in hand, running my eye over our stock. A hell of a lot of money was laid out there on the grass. There were two good longcase clocks we'd paid a considerable amount for. Both were well proportioned, with arched dials and good figured mahogany cases; assembled they were impressive pieces of furniture, but lying there, their hoods propped against the wall and their works carefully packed in cardboard boxes, they looked quite pathetic. I carried the two boxes of works into the shop and set them under the counter, for Baz was not the gentlest of furniture removers.

The signwriting was the worst I had ever seen in my life. Blood-red lettering in a variety of sizes and thicknesses covered the entire side of the blue van: 'F. Frank esq. houses cleared, shipping goods and antiques bought and sold. Purveyor of Object D'Arts.'

A small black-haired man stood looking down at the clock cases; his hands were thrust deep into his trouser pockets and he was whistling loudly. He raised his head as I approached and gave me a wide grin.

'Nice gear, guv.' His face was nut brown, two bright mischievous eyes met mine. There was more than a touch of the Romany about him. What he lacked in stature he made up for in colour and variety. His waistcoat of vivid hunting pink sported a huge gold guard chain and every finger carried its gold ring. He wore almost white moleskin trousers tucked into tooled-leather cowboy boots, and a crimson neckerchief disappeared into a grimy checked shirt.

He picked his way through the furniture, commenting on every piece. He pulled the drawers out of the chest-on-chest,

27

carefully examined all the dovetails, ran his fingers along the cornice and compared the back boarding in the two pieces.

'It's a right 'un, guv,' he called over his shoulder as he went on to pick up a Windsor chair.

The back doors of the van opened and a huge, fat girl wearing a long dirty caftan and even dirtier plimsolls dropped heavily to the ground.

'Hey, Little Petal! Come and look at this gear,' shouted the man. She completely ignored him and, brushing her black greasy hair from her face, she waddled down to the wash-fold, sat on a fallen stone and plunged her plimsolled feet into the icy beck. With her hands cupped each side of her fat face she sat motionless, watching the water swirl around her ankles. There was no hint of waistline or bust under the dirty brown garment.

The little man, his inspection complete, came and sat on the wall beside me. 'Good gear, but a bit up market for me. It's your shipping stuff I'm after.' I had bought a good oak mirror-back sideboard some weeks previously and I led him to where it lay sheeted up under the Dutch barn. He stood in front of it, hands in pockets, whistling. 'Well, what's it to be, guv?' he said presently.

I told him the price I wanted. He stood running his eyes over it for a good two minutes. Could I do it a bit better? I didn't know if we were on one of his regular routes or if he was just a chance caller we would never see again, but I had already found I could buy shipping furniture up the dales quite reasonably and was keen to build up a nucleus of regular callers. I knocked ten pounds off the original price. It was cheap and he knew it.

'That's the death is it, guv?'

'That's the death, Mr Frank,' I replied.

He turned and grinned up at me. 'Call me Fiery, guv. Everybody calls me Fiery.'

We loaded the mirror-back into the van. Vicky brought two mugs of coffee and a plate of biscuits and set them on the wall.

'Would your girlfriend like some coffee?' she enquired.

'No, doesn't like it, but she likes biscuits,' Fiery replied.

Vicky took the plate of biscuits down to the wash-fold and held it out towards Little Petal. Without saying a word, the girl took the plate and laid it in the grass beside her. Vicky looked a little nonplussed.

'Doesn't say a lot,' ventured Fiery, 'but she's a bugger in bed. When she's that way out she bounces me about like a bloody rag doll.'

Vicky tried to hide her laughter and hurried into the shop. I could hear her muffled giggles coming from the shop as Fiery counted out the money on to the wall. He called Little Petal and she slopped her way silently up the green. Placing the empty plate in my hand, she heaved herself into the van. She had sat with her feet in the cold beck for almost an hour.

Fiery started the engine and wound down the window. 'We come through here about once a month, always on the lookout for a bit of shipping gear.'

'Where are you from?' I asked.

'Black Pudding Land,' he shouted back, grinning widely.

Vicky was still laughing when I got back to the shop. 'He says they are from Black Pudding Land.' I must have looked puzzled.

'Lancashire, he means Lancashire,' she replied.

*

29

By the time The Ship was open Baz and I had all the furniture set around the shop, pictures hung from the walls, and the till sat, empty bellied, on the counter.

We were open for business.

When you open a shop you invite the world and his wife to come through your door and in the antique trade, as in any other, you try to build up a regular clientele. Someone once wrote that a collector was among the happiest of men, and to a certain degree this is true. If one specializes in gold snuff boxes by Fabergé the field is somewhat limited, but lesser mortals, content with militaria, Staffordshire figures or even the humble cigarette card, can hunt happily through every antique shop, auction room and church bazaar. The most unpromising of sources can yield unexpected treasure. I once bought three Victorian fairings for ten pence each at a boy scouts' jumble sale.

As a collection is built up over the years, the little stories attached to each acquisition accumulate into a tapestry of memories as evocative as any well-kept diary. A true collector will live on bread and water to get his hands on a desirable piece, and his fervour can be raised to an unbelievable pitch when battling against a rival in a sale.

Once, on a hot afternoon in August, I was sitting at the back of an auction room. There were a hundred or so lots to be sold before anything came up that was of interest to me. The sun streamed through the upper windows as I lay back against a chiffonier and resigned myself to an hour of boredom. The auctioneer droned on through an assortment of jewellery, until he came to a fine Georgian verge watch. There was a lot of interest in it and the hubbub of conversation died away as the price rose.

A small bespectacled man in the front row was bidding against the Ring. He stared fixedly at the auctioneer, and grew more and more agitated as the bidding climbed well over the market value. Finally he shook his head and, rising from his seat, dashed the watch from the hand of the surprised steward and rushed out of the auction room.

Much to our relief, we did soon have a small body of regular customers. The first tourists of the season were also beginning to throng the dale, and it looked as if the economics of the shop would be viable. Several of the locals began to patronize us regularly and, although not violent, they could still be very difficult. Mrs Smythe-Robinson collects cranberry glass. A large, self-confident woman, she is the leading member of half a dozen ladies' clubs. She is always immaculately turned out and always demands a lot of attention. I had spent half an hour trying to sell her a really good Victorian epergne, when I heard the screech of Fiery Frank's van pulling into the yard.

I'm afraid I haven't the patience that Vicky has with customers. I feel that if the article is sound, genuine and reasonably priced, they should part with their money and leave gracefully. This morning I had given of my best; I'd taken all the vases and shepherds' crooks out of the base of the epergne, one by one, for Mrs Smythe-Robinson to inspect, but the lady was not in one of her best moods. As always she was impeccably dressed, in a beige two-piece well tailored to her ample figure. She wore a fox fur stole of the type popular a quarter of a century ago, and a hat which would not have disgraced any Conservative Party conference. Taking the base of the epergne to the window, she turned it slowly in the light. It was a particularly nice colour. The piece was not overpriced by any means, but, although her husband was a wealthy quarry owner, the lady still held her purse strings tightly.

'Yes,' she said finally. 'I'll take it.' I reached under the counter for the sheets of tissue – no newspaper for the carriage trade. I had three of the vases carefully mummified in paper, when Fiery burst into the shop.

'Morning, guv. Any new gear?' He eyed Mrs Smythe-Robinson from top to bottom, obviously taken with the fox stole. 'By gum, you've a hairy chest, missus.'

The door bell jangled furiously behind the irate woman. I unwrapped the vases and smoothed out the expensive tissue paper. 'Thanks very much, Fiery.'

'It's OK, guv. See you round the back.' Fiery hesitated at the door. One of the fox tails from Mrs Smythe-Robinson's stole was jammed firmly in it. He retrieved it and handed it to me with a cheeky grin. 'A trophy of the chase, guv.'

I had lost a good sale that morning, but I knew Fiery always tried to buy. We had done a part house clearance and some of the stuff was right in Fiery's line. There was a 1920s walnut bedroom suite I knew he would find irresistible; it would just be a matter of the eternal haggling.

Little Petal waddled off to sit in the orchard, as Fiery and I mounted the steps to the apple house. She was wearing a full, billowing white dress patterned with huge blue irises. It looked suspiciously like curtain material to me.

Fiery was on form; he had money in his pocket. We carried the bedroom suite into the yard, a hall-stand and a commode soon followed with a nice pair of spelter figures. I'd hung an Afghan jezail from one of the rafters; it was a flintlock crudely inlaid with mother-of-pearl and brass wire. They were terrible weapons, as dangerous to the firer as the intended victim, but they sold well as pub decorations. Known in the trade as 'gas pipe guns', the usual practice was to rod them to make sure no charge had been left in, but as I'd rodded dozens and found nothing I'd never bothered to do this one. Fiery took it down from the rafter. He was obviously taken with it so I quoted him a fairly stiff price. The incident with Mrs Smythe-Robinson still rankled. Fiery shuddered and laid it on top of a chest of drawers. We carried down a pair of inlaid bed ends and a good oleograph of a horse fair, and laid them with the furniture. Sitting on the steps, I totted up Fiery's bill and handed it to him. He counted out the money and, starting to roll the spelter figures in blankets, he called Little Petal. As Fiery and I fed the furniture into the van Little Petal packed it carefully, her great weight rocking the vehicle as she passed from side to side. Stronger than most men, she pushed and heaved the furniture until it nested together, carefully placing old army blankets between the polished surfaces. Fiery stood watching her, his hands thrust deep into his trouser pockets.

'Sixty quid any good for the artillery?'

I had quoted him seventy for the jezail but he'd been a good buyer and it was always cash. I nodded my head in agreement and Fiery bounded up the steps to fetch it.

'Wrap this up, luv,' he said, dropping the gun on the van floor.

The explosion was terrific. Little Petal shrieked and stumbled, sobbing, from the smoke-filled van. Clutching her left buttock with one hand, she swung a hefty punch at Fiery with the other. The little man staggered back across the yard under its impact. He regained his balance and mounted the apple house steps in two magnificent bounds.

'You stupid little bastard,' screamed Little Petal as she made after him, tears streaming down her ample cheeks. Fiery slammed the door behind him and wedged a chair under the handle. Little Petal heaved herself up the steps and hammered on the door; between sobs and groans she hurled a tirade of abuse at Fiery, so laced with obscenities it would have delighted a cavalry sergeant. The blue iris had completely disappeared from her left buttock, exposing an area of bruised and blackened skin twice the size of a man's hand.

Vicky and I half carried her into the kitchen and leaned her over the pine table. Peter poked a wide-eyed face around the door.

'What was that big bang, Daddy?' This brought on a fresh bout of sobbing which shook the table.

I shooed the boy out and beat a gentlemanly retreat, as Vicky rubbed face cream into the huge bruise.

Fiery peered nervously from the apple house window.

'Is she all right?' he asked in a weak voice.

'She's all right,' I told him, 'but I'll give you one guess which orifice she's going to insert that jezail into.'

Fiery groaned. 'She gets a bit violent at times, guv. I have to be fleet of foot.'

I recalled the little man's ascent of the steps and smiled.

None of Vicky's dresses would fit the girl, so after treating the injury as best we could we pinned a tablecloth around her. I unpacked the commode and set it at the back of the van. Little Petal gingerly lowered herself into it, twisting sideways to favour the injured part. Only when she was fully settled in with an ample supply of biscuits did Fiery venture forth from the apple house. The van still smelled acrid from the black powder as I closed the rear doors on Little Petal. I held my hand out in front of the pale Fiery.

'Sixty quid.' He peeled out the notes and climbed into the cab.

'*Bon voyage*,' I called cheerfully. Little Petal's voice had the deep measured vehemence in it only an injured woman can achieve.

'I'll give the little bugger *bon voyage* when I get him home.'

Fiery was not the only shipping dealer to start calling on us. Colin soon put it about where we were and made us some good contacts, and wherever I could I turned the van up the dale in search of stock.

We had started advertising our wants in the local press and this brought a steady trickle of replies. Some were time wasters, but we still managed to buy quite well. Pine had not yet reached its zenith and many a barn yielded a good press or meal ark. We found that placing postcards in the windows of village shops was quite productive, and the children carefully printed us a supply of cards which we carried in the glove compartment.

I pulled up at the Middlethwaite Post Office, a neatly printed card in my hand, and as usual read all the other cards in the window before I went in. Sometimes that 'old washstand' or 'big table' could prove quite interesting. The card which caught my eye was barely legible. Where it touched the glass, condensation had blurred the ink and the scrawly writing had a pale blue halo around each letter: 'Stone troffs and garden seets for sale. Apply Davy Banks evenings.'

The postmistress smiled as I asked after Mr Banks. 'No, no, dear, that's the place. It's Long John you want.' Her instructions were clear and concise. 'Down through the village, second left before the beck and keep going as far as you can.'

*

The track rose steeply, the wheels slipping then biting on the loose pebbles. From the size of the grass verge on each side it had obviously been a drove road. It was cut with a deep rain channel which coursed from side to side, sending the van rocking and banging the springs to their limits. As the track levelled off, the drystone walls stopped abruptly and the land fell away steeply to the right. To the left, short grass crept among clumps of rounded gorse, before both gave way to gently undulating heather. Black-face sheep raised inquisitive heads and grouse rose on whirring wings to dip and swoop out of sight.

The good postmistress had said 'keep going' and keep going I did, for nowhere was it possible to turn round. The track was just the width of one vehicle and the lie of the land at each side was too steep to allow any manoeuvre. The track started to descend, and in the distance I could see several white goats tethered each side of it. Ahead lay a group of low buildings huddling together under a fell side of scree and blackthorn.

Long John lived up to his name; almost six and a half feet tall, he was thin to the point of being scraggy. Heavily bearded, his pronounced stoop brought the beard half-way down his hollow chest, his arms were exceptionally long and his hands, large and muscular, had been reddened and cracked by the elements. His face, in contrast, had a waxy pallor. Where the skin tightened over the cheekbones it was almost luminous but the nose, thin and hooked, had caught the elements too, and a matrix of tiny exposed blood vessels gave it the match to his hands. His eyes were black, brooding, steady eyes, and if the close-cropped hair and full beard had been titian instead of the crow black they were, he would have been a living Van Gogh.

He wore a heavy checked shirt buttoned to the neck and ex-army trousers which were six inches too short, revealing one blue sock and one red. I felt I could do business with a man who could stand unselfconsciously in such socks.

'I've come about the garden seats and the troughs.' Long John nodded and, turning without a word, led me down the yard through a motley of hens, ducks and bantams to a pole barn.

The stone troughs were badly chipped and cracked, but the seats were fine – heavy cast-iron ends in the form of serpents, their forked tails curved elegantly behind the backrests while the heads rose to support the hands, flat-tongued mouths open to tempt the finger of a daring child.

There were four pairs of ends and, as I turned them over in the straw looking for damage, Long John kept up a stream of questions. I did not want to show too much enthusiasm for the seats so I inspected the unwanted troughs just as carefully. By the time I had finished, Long John knew a good deal more about me than I about him. A cattle dealer by trade, he enjoyed the haggling. Leaning back against one of the pole supports, he drew heavily on a hand-rolled cigarette. We finally settled on a price which neither of us was particularly pleased with, and I reversed the van down the steep yard. The questions continued as we loaded the heavy castings. I answered them all frankly and good-naturedly, for I liked the man.

The yard was a tip. Old tyres and rotting bales of straw were half sunk in mud. Poultry picked their way through a tangle of rusting machinery and pigeons lined the roof of the sad-looking house. At the top of the yard stood an irregular row of old vans, each one discarded as it failed its MOT. A trio of geese hissed their antagonism from the back of a wheel-less Morris.

'I put them in when I saw you coming,' explained Long John. 'They're buggers for legs.'

Evening was drawing on and a black rain cloud hung over the fell, the first big drops splatting into the mud as I paid for the seat ends. He looked like being a good contact so I took one of our old cards and, writing the pub phone number on it, handed it to him. His head bent even further on to his chest as he stared at it.

Vicky would be wondering where I'd got to – I had gone up the dale to deliver a set of chairs when I'd seen the card in the Post Office window. The goats turned their backs to the approaching storm as I bumped down the track. I could see Long John in the mirror; oblivious of the grey rain which now swept the yard, he stood there still staring at the card. I think he has a little trouble with the written word.

A fortnight passed before we heard from Long John. The message was short and to the point: 'Got some gear in your line.'

Vicky and the children insisted on coming with me. It was a mild sunny evening, so we left the dogs tied in the yard. The track was even more treacherous than before; recent rains had freshly scoured the gullies and the children held tightly to the backs of our seats as we bumped and jolted our way to Long John's.

He must be expecting us, I thought as we pulled into the yard, for the geese had been safely shut in the Morris. He was nowhere to be seen. I knocked long and loud on the farmhouse door. Getting no response, I eased the door open. Two sheep curs leapt snarling from a wrecked settee. I slammed the door quickly and we went to search the barns.

We found Long John in his workshop – a corrugated-tin shed

38

built out from the stone barn, two concrete pillars supporting it where the banking fell away. A ten-foot-diameter water-wheel turned merrily at one side, sending spumes of water over the rusted sheeting.

Long John looked up and grinned as we entered. 'I have to get stuck in while there's enough water,' he explained. He was squatting on a small stool in front of a huge buffing wheel. The floor was scattered with fire-irons, jampans and copper kettles. The buffer was geared up from the water-wheel shaft by a series of pulleys and belts and the whole shed trembled to the steady rumble of the wheel. The children looked on in awe as Long John rose to his full height; even with his stoop his hair brushed the tin roof.

'I see you've brought the bairns. Do they like horses?' Sally and Peter nodded silently. Long John picked his way through the brass and copper to the door. His long arm pointed up the yard. 'If you go in that stable there you'll find Polly. There's some tack on the wall, can you fettle a horse?' Both shook their heads. 'Well, your mother had better take you while me and your dad have a look at some stuff.'

Polly was a black Dales mare. Rising ten, she was as quiet as an old sheep. Vicky saddled and bridled her and led her on to the track with two excited children following behind.

Long John had assembled his goods down the centre of the dark barn. It took a while for my eyes to become accustomed to the gloom. All of it was good commercial stuff and anything that would not go in the shop was in Fiery Frank's line. I had a relatively easy passage buying it. Long John quoted reasonable prices and any haggling was purely nominal. We loaded the van and Long John led me back to his workshop. The red-socked foot swept the centre of the floor clear and he lifted a small trapdoor. A stone-lined cavity under the floor housed a small spirit-fired still. His long arm reached down and he brought up a small stainless-steel can filled with a clear liquid.

Pouring its contents into two mugs, he passed one to me. 'Here's to a good deal and many more.' The mugs clanked together and I raised mine cautiously to my lips. I took the slightest of sips and pressed my tongue to the roof of my mouth. It did not burn instantly but diffused quickly through-out the mouth, causing me to gasp. The sharp intake of breath made me cough and soon I was bent over the buffing frame, eyes streaming and saliva trickling from my open mouth. Long John laughed. 'Good stuff, eh?'

'What the hell is it?' I gasped.

'Swaledale Lightning, son, the elixir of life.' He took the mug from my hand and, opening the small window, held it under the spume from the water-wheel until it filled to the brim. Handing the mug back he concentrated his huge frame on to the small stool. 'Good for all ailments the flesh is heir to. I haven't had a cold for ten years. If I feel a bit of a chill coming on, half a mugful with some black pepper stirred in does the trick. It cures the ague, palsy and the flying squitters, and a fit of depression flies before it like a leaf on the wind.'

Diluted as it was, it took some drinking. I squatted on the shed floor as Long John, elated with the liquor, recounted his life story. Dusk was gently painting out the distant hills as Polly clopped her way back to the stable under a double load. She was patted and thanked and rubbed down with wisps of straw. I suggested that Vicky should drive, and with a full van settled myself into the passenger seat with an excited child on each knee.

As we pulled out of the yard, Long John hurried out of the house and waved us to stop. He opened the passenger door and thrust a bottle on to the seat beside me. Vicky eased the van down the track to the main road.

'The dogs will be going mad, they've never been tied up for so long.'

'Stuff the dogs,' I replied quietly, grinning up at the van roof.

We put the bottle of Swaledale Lightning on the highest stone shelf in the dairy, against the day when we might be visited by the ague, palsy or the flying squitters.

We were working five days a week on the shop, and would slump into our beds at night to sleep the sleep of the just.

The only thing that ever kept us from our slumbers was the wind; it would sweep down from the fell and shriek and moan around the caravan, before sending the dustbin rattling across the yard. It was a feature of the dale; it was why every house had its porch and every garden its windbreak. Its fiendish fingers stroked every roof and every tree as it passed, looking for the loose tile and the weak branch. We would lie in bed staring at the roof of the caravan, listening.

On the first day of April, a late fainthearted snowfall had powdered the yard all day and a fresh breeze, twisting and playing, had sent cats' paws of snow under the caravan to lie in white collars around the jacks and wheels. I had been chipping old plaster from the byre walls all day, and I lay in bed with aching arms and a neck so stiff I could find no comfort no matter how I shuffled the pillows. Vicky and the children were hard asleep. The wind rose steadily. I heard the dog bowls rattle down the yard, and listened to the steady clack-clack of Ted's garden gate as the wind toyed with it. Sleep would not come.

I watched the luminous hands of the little travelling clock creep into the early hours. Now the wind was gusting, and I lay worrying about the caravan; we had supported it well but had done nothing to hold it down.

I donned a dressing gown and wellingtons, and drove the van upwind of the caravan to form a windbreak. As I jumped down from the cab I ducked instinctively, as the lean-to tore away from the caravan and, with a rending and crashing, hurtled down the yard, disintegrating as it went. The gas bottle rolled after it, flailing its rubber pipe and hissing out its contents.

It was four o'clock in the morning when I sank on to the bed and, still in dressing gown and wellingtons, fell into a deep sleep.

Vicky had got a fire going in the old range, and I awoke to the smell of bacon and eggs. She had pulled off my wellingtons and wrapped an eiderdown around me and as I tucked into breakfast she sat on the edge of the bed and recounted the morning's news. The Colonel's greenhouse had blown down, the road to Lalbeck was blocked with a fallen tree and the chapel fence had blown away. We'd come off pretty lightly. The only real damage was two huge gouges down the side of the caravan, where the corrugated-iron roof of the lean-to had caught it.

'And,' Vicky added with a smile, 'we have lost several items of clothing.'

'Several items of clothing?'

'Yes, I've got everything back from the washing line except your best shirt and my black bra and panties.'

My best shirt we never found, but Vicky's bra and panties appeared the next day draped elegantly on the wash-fold. Old

Mr Hall stationed himself on the seat opposite and brought them to the attention of everybody.

'Are they yours, missus?' he asked every woman who passed.

The reactions he got varied: some laughed, some sniffed indignantly and some completely ignored him, but his wide toothless grin never failed. It was one of the best days of his retirement.

Chapter 4

Every dealer dreams of a big find. As he daily works his way through mundane commercial wares, his mind is often on higher things – the Constable lying undiscovered in some loft, a superb Etruscan bronze being used as a doorstop, the Ming vase nestling in a box of household goods at a cottage sale. One such find and he can eat the bread of idleness for the rest of his days. There are finds to be made, but they are invariably of a much lesser degree. As goods are getting more and more difficult to acquire, every auction room is picked over, every fleamarket scoured and even the unlikeliest of advertisements followed up.

We had one of our best days at a farm dispersal sale. There is still a lot of good period oak coming out of dales farmhouses, and any reference in an auction advertisement to the effect that surplus furniture will be offered brings dealers from far and wide. Usually it results in a bevy of dealers jostling for two or three bits of furniture. 'More cats than mice', is the usual comment.

The farm had been tenanted by the same family for four generations. The present tenant, now well into his seventies, had hung on too long. The son who should have taken over twenty years ago lay in a grave somewhere in North Africa. I'd seen his photograph hanging on the kitchen wall – a tall, gangly youth looking uncomfortable in khaki, staring unsmiling at the camera, one of the hundreds of young dalesmen who had flocked to the colours. The old man and his wife could no longer cope. The long years had taken their toll; bent backs and arthritic limbs had made them long for the little warm cottage in the village. He'd hung on because there had been a Dinsdale at Kebblestones for nearly two hundred years.

He leaned over the yard wall, silently watching as his small dairy herd came under the hammer one by one. His wife stood beside him, a small neat woman with iron-grey hair pulled back in a tight bun. She had on a freshly ironed pinny and constantly toyed with its strings. The cows were all past their best and the bidding was tardy.

The furniture had all been set out in the front garden, with the exception of a small Georgian bureau which stood in the hallway. We'd viewed it earlier in the morning and I sat on the yard wall while Vicky and Sally wandered around the farm with the dogs. Peter had volunteered for the job of clerk's runner and stood rigidly by his side, waiting for each sales sheet. As soon as one was handed down to him he ran, weaving his way through the crowd, to the cashier who had set up office in the farmhouse kitchen. It was a job that could be worth a pound or two on a good sale day.

The last milk beast was prodded and thwacked into the yard. It stood head down, its lower lip drooping, its huge pelvic bones standing out on its hindquarters and every rib showing down

its flanks. It had come to the end of its lactation and the auctioneer announced that it was 'dry'. He looked across at the
farmer for confirmation and the old man nodded his head. It
should have been culled from the herd years ago, but it had
always been a good milker and an easy calver and the old man
had kept it on.

'It'll bull again,' the auctioneer called encouragingly.

'You'll have to find a very gentle bull,' came back a shout
from the crowd.

Everybody laughed except the old man and his wife. It was
finally sold to a manufacturing butcher for the lowest price of
the day. It was pushed and bullied up the ramp of the cattle
wagon to be taken away from the farm for the first time in its
seventeen years.

The sheep which were not hefted to the upland pastures
were driven into the yard. Still with their lambs at foot, the ewes
were sold in batches of six. Two wild-eyed dogs circled them
continually, lolling tongues almost touching the dusty yard. I
had no interest in the sheep and wandered into the big stone
barn.

It was cold and quiet after the noisy yard and I was glad to
be away from the mass of flies the sheep had brought with
them. The barn was half floored and sweet-scented hay was
stacked to the eaves. The thick layers of whitewash softened the
rough facing of the stones and eyebrows of dust hung over each
protrusion. Near the apex of the roof, where the adzed beams
closed on the ridge-piece, owl holes were set in the walls, proof
that the barn had been built at a time when corn was grown in
the upper dales. Cobwebs and dust lay thick on the high
window ledges, covering discarded drenching horns and
cartwheel hub spanners. The floor was uneven, big riverbed

cobbles worn smooth with the passage of hooves and yard-brush were set in lime mortar. The joints between the cobbles had eroded away and a matrix of hay lay in them like a giant hairnet.

This was the heart of the farm. Solid and dependable, it had weathered a thousand storms. Its thick stone walls and flagged roof had protected the hardwon hay and sheltered the valuable stock. The product of countless sweated hours had rested safe here. It had been the scene of numerous victories and numerous tragedies. The difficult calvings when carbolic-scrubbed arms had fought to turn the calf and bring it safely out to lie wet and gangly-legged beside its mother. The sickening beast, failing to respond to vet and quack remedy alike, felled and dragged out by the knacker's man. The old farmer had been milking in here when the red Post Office bike had throbbed into the yard; the pale buff telegram – 'His Majesty's Government regrets to inform you . . .' He'd pressed his head into the beast's warm flank, tears had coursed down his leathery cheeks and dropped silently to mingle with the milk.

They were selling the last of the sheep, two huge tups. Black-faced with pronounced Roman noses, they turned to face the dogs and stamped angry feet. The furniture was to be sold next so I stood at the back door of the farmhouse. Peter hurried past me importantly, ignoring me. There is more than a little of the theatre in all auctions and he had a role to play. The tups fetched high prices. They were from well-known bloodlines and their progeny were among the best in the dale.

'We'll sell the furniture now, then the implements and produce.' The auctioneer dropped heavily from his box.

The cattle men and the sheep men gathered in little groups. Men funnelled through the hallway to the front garden. I tailed in behind the auctioneer and his clerk. He stopped when he came to the bureau. 'Let's sell this desk thing.' The steady stream of men stopped and turned to face him. 'A hundred? Well, fifty.' I raised my hand and the cane swung to point at me. 'Sixty, is there sixty for the desk?' A tall, red-faced man in a blue boiler suit pushed up to the bureau, turned his head and nodded to the auctioneer. The cane flicked towards him and back to me. I nodded. 'Seventy, eighty, ninety.' The cane flicked back and forth at each bid. Boiler Suit shook his head. 'Ninety pounds here.' The cane slapped on the bureau and the crowd turned and surged into the garden.

I gave my card to the clerk and started to take the drawers out of the bureau. I couldn't get it in the van fast enough. Boiler Suit stood behind me, watching. 'Tha'll find no sovereigns in there, mate. Sid's a tight bugger.'

I smiled at him and carried a chin-high pile of drawers out to the van. Even without the drawers the carcass was heavy, and I half dragged, half 'walked' it to the back door.

'Do you want a lift?' enquired Boiler Suit.

I thanked him as we slid it on to the van floor and set to work putting back the drawers. It was an unnecessary task as I would have to take them out again when we got home, but I wanted to see it together again. All the handles were original and it had a neat stepped interior. It was a good size, a little under three feet, and the colour was superb. I wrapped it carefully in blankets and roped it to the van side.

I locked the van carefully; the Ring would not be pleased and it was not unknown for a drawer or a handle to go missing from a piece of furniture when they were thwarted.

The Ring was not a fixed entity. It had a permanent nucleus of two or three dealers, who would approach the other major

48

dealers before an auction. 'Do you want to be in?' they would ask. Those that did would join the little gang and let the 'front man' do the bidding for them, content in the knowledge that there would be rich pickings for them in the 'knock-out', when the goods were auctioned again amongst themselves and the difference between the old and the new prices shared out equally.

I couldn't wait to find Vicky and tell her my good news. It was the best buy we had ever had.

Vicky was sitting on the garden wall. 'Where have you been?' she asked anxiously. 'The Ring is taking everything decent.' I told her about the bureau and she smiled. 'That'll not please them.'

Sally pushed her way between us and turned her face up to me. 'Fatty Batty is buying for the Ring,' she piped in a loud voice.

Fatty must have heard her for he turned and scowled at us. The rest of the Ring, six of them, were at the bottom of the garden, talking loudly and laughing amongst themselves. The current lot was a pine dresser base which did not interest us, so Vicky took the opportunity to tell me which furniture had sold and what it had fetched. There were a lot of private buyers and the Ring had not got anything really cheap.

Next to be sold was a Victorian camel-back sofa. Mahogany-framed, it still had its original horsehair covering. It was the type hated by generations of short-trousered schoolboys, for the ends of the hairs pricked like needles into the backs of bare legs. I worked my way through the crowd to behind the auctioneer, where I could see Fatty. The sofa was a nice piece and the bidding was brisk. The auctioneer was on the point of knocking down to Fatty when I called loudly, 'Here.' I wanted

Fatty to know it was me. I took him on for another four bids before I shook my head. Fatty glowered.

As the crowd moved round the garden I kept Fatty in sight. When something was being sold which did not interest the Ring Fatty took the opportunity to try to hide himself in the crowd, but if I lost sight of him Vicky, now standing on the wall, would point him out. The auctioneer soon realized what was happening and every time Fatty was the last bidder he turned to me before knocking it down. Every time I made Fatty go another two or three bids. He never had a lot of colour, but his plump face was now quite red.

I dogged him to the end of the furniture sale. The crowd filed through a little gate into the field where the implements were set in long rows.

'What about the bureau?' Fatty called to the auctioneer.

'Sold it,' came the curt reply from the clerk.

Fatty marched down the garden. The Ring gathered around him in silence. There were no rich pickings today.

I had got the bureau at a fraction of its value due to the incompetence of the auctioneer, but I'd more than compensated the Dinsdales for it. I'd taken hundreds of pounds from the Ring and put the proceeds in their pocket.

Vicky had bought one lot while I'd been away, a trayful of glasses. She set to work carefully wrapping them in newspaper as I went to pay the cashier. He sat in the kitchen at an oilcloth-covered table writing out the bills in a neat clerk's hand. Behind him stood an oak bacon settle.

'That's not for sale,' he said without lifting his head, as I ran my fingers over it. A nice simple piece of dales furniture, it was of the usual panelled construction but the doors, instead of opening from the front as normal, were set in the back. Had it been made as a free-standing piece to be pulled up to the fire, making the rear doors accessible, or was it to set against a wall, so affording maximum security to the precious flitches? The front and sides were highly polished but the back was as dry as the day it was made. It was the only piece of furniture the Dinsdales were taking with them. I paid the cashier and we sat in the van waiting for Peter. He was still busy, running from the field to the kitchen with every newly filled sales sheet. Vicky searched through the cardboard box of glasses. There was one she particularly wanted me to see. It was a small trumpet-shaped wine glass with a folded foot and heavily knopped stem. Engraved on the glass was the word 'FIAT' and opposite it a rose flanked by two rosebuds. The flowers represented James I, his son and his grandson. With the bureau and the Jacobite glass we had had a good day. Peter returned, happily clutching two crisp pound notes, and we set off home in high spirits.

It was early evening and we were hungry and tired, but happy. As we passed through Middlethwaite the pub was just opening so I swung into the car-park. It wasn't a typical dales pub; it had changed hands recently and the new owners had their own idea of how a country pub should be. The old planked bar had been torn out and replaced with a stone one, copper-topped and carrying a bewildering array of illuminated beer dispensers. Reproduction horsebrasses hung from plastic beams and a simulated log fire flickered unconvincingly from the random stone fireplace. The outside had not escaped the improvers: a stone-flagged patio was set with tables and benches and an old Scotch cart, painted white with flame-red wheels, carried its load of potted flowers. I left Vicky and the children dividing up the crisps and carried my beer across to the van. I opened the back doors and took the blankets off the bureau. I'd been sitting on the wheel arch looking at it for no more than a minute or two when a slick Mercedes estate swept into the car-park. It was Fatty Batty.

His eyes fixed on the bureau as he slowed the car to a walking pace. His white moon face turning to fill the side window, he drove slowly past the open doors of the van. There was a sickening crunch as the bonnet of the car nosed under the flower-laden cart, which lurched forward off its props scattering half a dozen pots of flowers against the windscreen. The cartwheels, rotten under the glossy new paint, collapsed gracefully, spilling the rest of the flowers in a colourful heap on the ground.

What the new landlord lacked in taste he more than made up for in size. Fatty was carefully picking the plants from his car as he emerged from the pub, white with rage.

We'd never liked Fatty, he was arrogant and greedy, but I felt quite sorry for him as we climbed into the van and left him, pot of primulas in hand, silently enduring the wrath of the giant landlord. He had not had a good day.

Chapter 5

Part of our plan was to produce as much of our own food as possible. On the little land we had self-sufficiency was out of the question, not only because of the capital required to intensify it sufficiently, but because it would be far too time-consuming. We did agree, however, that we could easily produce our own eggs, vegetables and meat. We were intending to buy half a dozen point-of-lay pullets but Ted, our down-to-earth neighbour, talked us out of this. What we needed were old battery hens. They were cheap and, once acclimatized to free range, would produce eggs economically for a year and still not be too old for the pot. His arguments made sense.

The two-seater earth closet would make an admirable hen house; its thick stone walls and flagged roof would keep it warm in winter and cool in summer. We boarded over the two neat round holes, jammed a rough-hewn perch between the walls and, with a nine-inch-square hole cut in the bottom of the door, it only needed a fresh coat of whitewash. The children donned oilskins and goggles as Vicky mixed the whitewash and

I made a temporary pen in front of the closet. Ted lent us a stirrup-pump-type spray which clamped on to the bucket and the children took turns at pumping and spraying until both were completely covered in whitewash and a steady milky stream poured under the door and inched its zigzag way down the yard. I swept out the closet and propped the door wide open to let the wind dry it out. Baz stared at the whitened mud. 'I see ye've been bug blinding.'

As Vicky washed the children I walked across to the pub to telephone the poultry farm. 'Would you sell us as few as six of your old hens?'

'I'll sell you one if you want,' came the lugubrious reply, 'but you must bring your own crates, I have no crates. Everybody expects me to have crates.'

I assured him we would bring a crate. Vicky fetched two strong cardboard boxes from the shop and the children knelt on the floor in their pyjamas, punching holes in them with two screwdrivers. I set them under the lean-to ready for the next day, two square brown colanders each with its string handle.

We decided to fetch the hens in the early evening so that the children could come with us. Ted always gave his directions by means of pubs, so we duly passed The Black Swan and turned left at The Maypole. We bumped down the track for a hundred yards before the cottage came into view. Stone-built with a blue slate roof, its leaded windows caught the sunlight. A rustic porch covered in honeysuckle, now showing its first burst of leaf, guarded the front door. The path was bordered by a yellow froth of daffodils and the two squares of lawn, set symmetrically in front of the cottage, were of the deep verdant green seen only in a wet spring. To the left of the cottage a small man in a brown smock was hoeing neat rows of spring cabbage. He looked up as I clicked open the little gate.

'Have you brought a crate?' I assured him we had. Crates seemed to be a big worry in his life. Sally and Peter proudly held their perforated boxes as high as their little arms could manage. The man seemed unimpressed and, turning, led us behind the cottage.

Three huge battery houses stood on brick piers, their sliding doors wide open, and fans droned in their roofs. We walked past the first two houses and, although it was a mild evening, we could feel the heat as we passed each open door. Peering in we saw thousands of bobbing heads busy at the trough or nipple drinker.

The third house was half empty but the noise was still deafening. The cages stood four high and back to back in three enormous rows. There were four birds in each tiny cage. There were no feathers on their breasts, which were red and scaly, their limp combs fell over one eye and their tails were worn to the rump by constant contact with the cage. Several eggs lay on the narrow conveyor belt which collected them automatically. It was hot and stuffy, and the dust made our faces itch. Sally and Peter looked quite upset.

The man waved his arm along the cages. 'Pick yer own.'

Which six were we going to take out of all these thousands? Which six would cluck through our orchard, dustbathe in our yard and run to our back door for scraps? We finally decided to take one from each of the first six cages. I reached in, grabbed their thin struggling bodies and thrust them into the boxes.

There were over twenty thousand birds in the unit. Each battery house held birds of a different age; as one houseful came into full lay another was tapering off and so had to be disposed of. No doubt there was a graph somewhere on his office wall which charted the performance of each house. When the black line showing egg production drooped to touch the all-important red line of economics, it dictated the end for thousands of hens. Only a few were sold to people like us. The vast majority were stuffed into plastic crates and sent off to the processors in lorry-loads. They were hung upside down on monorails and electrically stunned, before being dragged through vats of boiling water and on to the plucking machines.

We bumped back up the lane in silence. We were all saddened by what we had seen.

'You will have to dig some worms for them and show them they have come to a good home,' I said. The children just sat staring at the boxes.

It was still daylight when we drove into the yard. I put the hens in the pen and the children set to work digging up worms. Peter manfully threw his over the pen but Sally proffered hers warily on a stick. The hens just squatted in a corner and completely ignored them. As night fell they were obviously not going to move, so I carried them into the closet and sat them on the perch. They promptly fell off. They had no strength in their claws to grip anything.

As we tucked the children into bed that night, Sally settled her head back on the pillow and stared at the caravan roof. 'I am never going to eat batteried eggs again as long as I live.'

Within a week the hens had changed enormously; their combs reddened, their legs became strong enough to perch and scratch and worms were much sought after. They had always been accustomed to contact with humans and were quite tame.

It was months before their feathers grew properly and we were a little ashamed of the bare reddened patches, but after their first moult a full brown plumage covered the whole of their bodies and we were quite proud of them – real barnyard fowl.

Ted was quite right, they never stopped laying. We never got the one egg per bird per day the man in the brown smock demanded from them, but they more than supplied our needs. Watercress was a favourite with them; they would patrol the banks of the beck, straining out their necks as far as they dared, for they were no lovers of water. Watercress is rich in iron, so the yolks were a deep rich orange. We delighted in giving surplus eggs to our friends and hearing their praise. Baz put it best: 'I haven't had eggs like these since I was a lad.'

Somehow I can't picture Baz as a lad, but Sally was right – we'd never eat batteried eggs again.

We were easily seduced away from the mundane tasks of house renovating, and the fine evenings of late spring would find us in the garden or garth, unless we had had a particularly hard day, then we just took the dogs and children and went to sit for an hour or so at the wash-fold.

I had taken the bacon flake down from the kitchen ceiling and the cheese traves from the dairy, scrubbing them and then stacking them carefully in the apple house. Fiery was particularly taken with the bacon flake. Every time he came to see us he tried to buy it, nodding into the corner where it stood – 'Come on, guv, let's be knowing' – but I never relented because it was one of the dales farmhouse features we were particularly keen on keeping.

Our attempts at food production were making progress. We had turned over most of the walled vegetable garden and the crops were coming along fine. Ted had brought round a trailer-load of manure and had supervised its digging in. 'You only get out what you put in,' he'd said solemnly.

With the hens giving us a steady stream of eggs it only left the question of milk. The goat is the cottagers' animal *par excellence*. Small and easily housed, they are efficient producers, giving more milk than the average household needs. Most of the popular conceptions about goats are unfounded. A mature billy-goat does give off an unpleasant aroma when in breeding trim, but a well-kept nanny gives no problem at all in this direction. Their milk is richer than that of a cow, has fewer fat globules, is entirely free of tuberculosis bacilli and carries more calcium. The problem is that a goat, like a cow, has to be milked twice a day, seven days a week, making it just as tying as a full-sized dairy herd.

Nevertheless, with all its drawbacks a goat had always fitted into our picture of life in the country. The best advice to any would-be goat owner is to buy a pedigree animal from a well-established breeder. With our usual propensity for ignoring good advice, we took ourselves off to Long John's when we heard he had a young nanny he might part with.

Long John kept several goats tethered on the verge of the steep track up to his cottage, where they had stripped the bark from, and thus killed, the elders and willows. Long John always kept white goats. They were healthy and milked well, but they had a spartan life and always seemed a little short of flesh. The rain was blowing in hard from the west as we trudged down the lane towards them. They stood in the lee of a drystone wall. We stopped opposite one which seemed slightly smaller than the rest.

'Good little goat that,' said Long John encouragingly. 'She

should be ready for the billy any time now.' I'd never been in the position of goat buyer before; I did not know what questions to ask or what to look for in the animal. We stood gazing at her for a long time, the children petted her and pulled handfuls of wet grass and thrust it under her pink muzzle.

'Comes of good milking stock,' said Long John, as I felt her little udder for lumps. Did goats suffer from mastitis? I had no idea. I looked at her feet, in her eyes, ears, nose and mouth; as far as I could ascertain she was a perfectly sound little animal.

'That's her mother,' said Long John, pointing at a big goat further down the lane. It was a much more substantial animal and had a longer coat, tinted with yellow, and a huge udder which thrust out from between her thin back legs. I asked him if this goat would grow as big. He avoided the question. 'Body size is nowt to go on,' he said, stroking his beard. Again the long arm waved out and pointed to a small goat further up the hill. 'That's the biggest milker I've ever had.'

We were not really worried about the quantity of milk; two or three pints a day was a sufficient quantity for our needs. More than anything, we wanted a quiet animal that was accustomed to being tethered. We wandered back up the lane. Although it was still driving with rain Long John didn't hurry and we were soaking wet by the time we reached the cottage. I had twice asked him how much he wanted for the goat but had received no answer. Still wearing his wet raincoat, he settled himself into an armchair. The children squatted in front of the log fire, steam rising from their wet clothes. They were already arguing about names for her; I knew I wasn't dealing from a strong hand. Again I asked him for the price.

'You can bring her back when she's ready for the billy.'

I had no intention of having her mated, for if she produced male offspring they would have no value and it was usual to knock them on the head at birth. This would be an impossible thing to do because of the children. I could see us over the years acquiring a useless herd of male goats. It is possible to bring the nanny to lactation by a simple injection.

'Well, what's it to be?' I asked again.

'Forty-five pounds,' came the reply.

'I'll give you forty and forget the billying.' This didn't seem to please Long John, who stared into the fire without replying. The children turned round and fixed me with solemn stares. I knew I was lost so I played my last card. 'We'll split the difference, forty-two pounds fifty.' There was still no reply. I stood feeling awkward in the silence, the children still staring at me. I looked to Vicky for support but she just smiled and shrugged her shoulders. There was nothing for it; I counted out nine five-pound notes on to the table. The children rose with a shout of glee, and hurried down the lane to fetch the goat.

'Bring the chain as well,' I shouted after them.

Long John rose with a little smile and went into the dairy. He reappeared with a bottle of Swaledale Lightning.

'Have a drop of that when tha gets home. It'll keep the cold out.'

It was still driving with rain as I lifted the little goat into the back of the van. The children squatted each side of it and patted it constantly.

'We've decided to call it Elspeth,' they chorused. Elspeth lifted her short tail and sent a stream of black droppings rattling on the van floor in approval.

Chapter 6

They say that in London every prostitute describes herself as a model and every pimp calls himself an antique dealer. There is no doubt that the trade harbours its share of charlatans, and when times are good new dealers appear like mushrooms. Most graduate into the trade from part-time dealing, but some take a heady plunge having sold off a successful business or inherited money, and without a solid background of knowledge to match their purchasing power.

The antiques trade can be a cruel shatterer of dreams. The pipe dream of a beautiful well-kept shop, gleaming with polished mahogany and Georgian brass and copper, is hard to realize and even harder to maintain. Time and again I've seen the high flier open his attractive shop packed with high-quality goods, then watched the steady decline in quality, usually ending up in stripped pine, before he finally closes the doors and takes to the antiques fairs circuit. The general public are fickle buyers, and good steady trade connections are essential. In winter sometimes many weeks can pass without the sale of a single item; the cash register is cold and still but the overheads march on. Bank managers are a sceptical breed of men and look with a jaundiced eye on second-hand car dealers and antique dealers alike. Apart from gambling, this is the fastest way I know to dissipate a fortune.

The Barracloughs were a sophisticated, middle-aged couple. He had been a senior executive in an international petro-chemical company and, taking the golden handshake after his second ulcer, had decided to achieve a lifelong ambition to become an antique dealer.

They purchased a beautiful Georgian building which had been an old alms house; its mellow hand-made brick and thin-leaded glass lancet windows made it the ideal setting. Standing in an acre of ground set with mature trees, it was renovated to a very high standard. The grounds were landscaped, a circular gravel drive laid, and the interior made into two large well-proportioned rooms with pastel walls and highly polished elm floors. They were seen in the major salerooms, always immac-ulately dressed, he with a clipboard – a sure sign of the amateur. They were lambs to the slaughter. They decided to specialize in Georgian oak and mahogany and the established trade, soon realizing this, fed them mercilessly. They seemed to have an inexhaustible amount of money.

We lesser mortals merely open our shops. Optimistically counting a float into the till, we unlock the door, turn the card to 'open' and nervously flick a duster over the stock. The Barracloughs however, accustomed to doing things in style, planned a grand opening. At the beginning of June the invita-tion arrived: a smart buff card with gold-embossed script requested the pleasure of our company on the appointed day.

The gathering was well attended, with a fair sprinkling of

dealers among a welter of friends and acquaintances. The sherry, brought round on galleried trays by uniformed maids, was superb. It was a grand affair. People mingled in a polite hubbub of conversation and lavished praise and admiration on everything. The setting was beautiful, the highly polished elm floor was strewn with Persian carpets and the furniture gleamed. In pride of place in the larger of the two rooms, which they had termed 'the long gallery', stood one of Arthur's fake refectory tables. It had been taken down to London and had come back to within fifteen miles of where it had been made. There was already a little red 'sold' ticket on it bearing the name of the lucky purchaser. They had stuck this over the price ticket and I was sorely tempted to peel this off, but good manners forbade.

Vicky and I wandered around looking at the furniture. A Georgian bureau-bookcase in a lovely golden oak with high patination carried a hefty price ticket. There was something odd about the proportions of the bookcase to the bureau itself. I withdrew a drawer and looked at the backboarding, which confirmed our suspicions. It was a marriage. Next to it stood a brass-faced longcase clock; its cherub spandrels pre-dated the case by a good eighty to one hundred years.

Vicky and I looked at each other and hurried round the rest of the furniture. Every piece was wrong. The coffer had a replacement lid; the mahogany gentleman's clothes press was a marriage; the two miniature chests of drawers had both had a recent association with the circular saw; the bachelor's chest hadn't housed its brushing slide long; the nice little rosewood chiffonier proudly carried a new bookcase top, complete with its brass gallery; and the impressive 'Regency' gilt and marble pier table hadn't long left the shores of sunny Italy, a country renowned for its quality faking of ornate furniture. A little thirty-hour cottage clock proudly showed its new brass face to the throng – this, too, bore a sold ticket; a large break-fronted bookcase which in its former days had guarded generations of clothes from the ravages of moths and time proudly carried an array of faked fairings and Staffordshire figures on its new shelves. One by one we went round each item of furniture, getting more and more bemused. Some were superb fakes, some were good marriages and some were plainly deplorable. Finally, we came to a small walnut davenport which had a circle of five or six dealers round it, all with glass in hand. It, too, carried a very handsome price ticket.

'Are you going to buy it?' said George.

'They give a good trade discount.' I smiled at him and we looked the piece over. Not only was it genuine, it bore the famous Gillows of Lancaster stamp which somewhat justified its price, as they were the originators of the davenport and always turned out articles of superb craftsmanship. The more we went over it the bigger the smiles on the dealers' faces became.

Alan Potts leaned forward and whispered confidentially in my ear, 'It's genuine.'

George guffawed. 'We've been discussing it and we've come to the conclusion that we shouldn't buy it because there ought to be at least one genuine piece in every antique shop.'

'How did it get here in the first place?' chipped in Fatty Batty.

George gave a look of mock bewilderment, 'We all make mistakes,' he explained. The gang burst out laughing. They had obviously made free with the sherry.

The Barracloughs, who were explaining the finer points of the wrong eight-day clock to a rich farmer and his wife, looked across and smiled. Things were going well for them. They had sold several high-priced pieces and they obviously misinterpreted the dealers' laughter. We felt quite embarrassed. As more and more free sherry was consumed, louder and more sarcastic remarks came from around the davenport. We edged away to examine a painting over the fireplace. Everybody was now looking at the little gang round the davenport.

'Let's buy it and cut the top off. Why shouldn't this little bugger have the saw into it like everything else?'

'I think it should have bracket feet.'

Comment followed comment, and each brought forth peals of laughter. George was now quite drunk. He staggered up to the Barracloughs. 'Whoever sold you that davenport wants his head examined.' He collapsed into a chair, helpless with laughter. Fatty Batty was sat on the floor, his glass between his feet, tears of laughter streaming down his face.

One of the dealers crawled up to Arthur's table, peeled off the sold ticket and peered at the price ticket underneath.

'Hey,' he called loudly, 'this Mr and Mrs Forbes must be a couple of right berks to have paid £2,500 for this.'

The Barracloughs looked hurt and bewildered. We never quite knew who Mr and Mrs Forbes were, but thought they must be the very smartly dressed couple with the quickly reddening faces.

We thanked the Barracloughs hastily and, choosing our words carefully, said, 'You have a lovely place here and we wish you every success.' We slipped out quickly. The boorishness of the gang appalled us; individually most of them were quite well off and well educated, but when they got together they drew strength from each other and became as a pack. Any outsider was fair game.

All the way home Vicky and I talked of nothing else but the amount of high-priced furniture the Barracloughs had sold on their opening day. They had taken more money in one day than we would take in a month, and yet every piece but one had something wrong with it. They were obviously sincere and honest people who had bought things in good faith and sold them in good faith. People had obviously taken them at face value; the superb setting and their sophisticated, middle-class background had caused people to believe implicitly in the authenticity of their goods. It could have been a big confidence trick but it wasn't. Their only mistake had been to move into a trade which is fraught with perils without gaining sufficient background knowledge. In a matter of months they had sold up and moved south, to take over a small private hotel.

The Radfords, in contrast, had worked their way steadily up the antique-dealing ladder, over many years. Starting on a Saturday market stall and graduating to fairs, they had acquired a good working knowledge and a basic feel for the trade before opening a modest shop. A rich vein of knowledge is also to be found in the saleroom and, if mined cautiously, much can be learned. The student must bear in mind, however, that the price achieved is not necessarily the value of the object. Some things can be ridiculously cheap, others absurdly expensive. We are often asked in a saleroom what a thing will fetch, my usual reply being, 'We can tell you what it is worth but not what it will fetch.'

The Radfords ploughed everything they had into their business. In the early years of their marriage they went without holidays and many of the electrical appliances deemed necessary by other young marrieds. They made mistakes, as everyone in this trade must. The old adage that one learns from one's mistakes is doubly true in the antiques business, where mistakes can be very, very expensive. The air-twist wine glass with folded foot borne home so proudly, on turning out to be a fake becomes an object of hate. The best course we have found is to put it immediately through the saleroom and employ the money returned to make good the deficit. The temptation to put it into a dark cupboard and forget it should be avoided – hanging on to it only compounds the error.

Gwen Radford specialized in fabrics. Fine lace would be hand washed in tepid water and gently air dried. An adept needlewoman, she repaired Victorian linen with loving care. On a visit to London she'd seen newly made nightdresses and nightshirts offered to the Americans as the genuine Victorian article.

'They were sewn entirely with modern nylon thread,' she told us indignantly. Richard and I made the appropriate clucking noises while Vicky shook her head in disbelief.

Gwen had nosed the flat iron in and out of the buttons on a velveteen cape, before inclining her head towards Vicky and continuing in a low voice, 'And I think they had originally been tablecloths.'

Both women had rolled their eyes in incredulity.

The Radfords had put off starting a family for many years, and were well established in their corner shop before little Caroline appeared. She was christened in a gown of cream satin trimmed with Bruges lace and embroidered with the coronet and cypher of a noble European house.

Richard was a self-taught cabinet maker and did work of a very high standard. He'd started life in the coal mines of South Yorkshire but, like so many of his colleagues in that shrinking industry, he was faced with redundancy. He retrained in a Government scheme as a joiner and there found his true love. Wood fascinated him; not the quick-grown kiln-dried soft woods of the North Americas he had had to work with while training, but the rich hard mahogany of the West Indies, the durable English oak and that most underrated of timbers, elm.

Richard had a phenomenal appetite for work and often burned the midnight oil. It was a joy to stand at the end of his bench on a cold winter's night and watch him form a cabriole leg for a Victorian nursing chair. With the heat from his well-fed stove pleasantly burning the backs of one's legs and the air filled with a rich cocktail of smells – glue, freshly sawn timber, beeswax and linseed oil – the time would fly by. Nothing would be said for long periods, but neither of us would feel awkward. The strong hands would dart about the bench and I would watch entranced as the blank piece of wood took shape.

Richard would straighten his back and smile. 'See to that glue, old lad.'

I would dutifully turn and stir the glutinous mass. 'Smooth as honey,' I would tell him.

He would bend to his work again. 'I've heard it called worse.'

His workshop was a converted coach-house and its apparent chaos was a deceit. Richard knew the whereabouts of everything. A long bench set with three vices occupied one entire side of the workshop and tiers of racks above it carried rows of gleaming chisels. After use, each chisel was stroked on the oil-stone and wiped with an oily rag before being returned to its proper place in the rack. His moulding planes were kept in drawers under the bench; hollows and rounds, roman ogee and thumb nail, the patterns were endless. Hand tools were his passion. The love and care he lavished on them contrasted sharply with the scant respect he showed for his power tools. A vintage hand-cranked bandsaw had been converted to electric power by a series of unguarded pulleys and flat belts which would have made a factory inspector shudder. Not for Richard the flash modern spindle moulder, every moulding, rule joint or readed panel was lovingly formed by hand. It was through his constant searching for different forms of moulding planes that we had first come to know him. We had bought the entire contents of a joiner's shop – a joiner of the old order.

Most of the planes were by Matheson of Glasgow and were high quality. Richard had spent hours going over them. Very politely he had asked permission to draw the blades. Sighting along the soles for wear and distortion, he weighed them in his hands. An expression we learned from him that day has stuck with us ever since: 'comes well to the hand,' he would say when one suited him. He graduated the planes in order of desirability, selected the few he could afford and nervously asked if we could keep some by for a week or so until he had more money. We agreed, of course, and eventually he bought the whole collection. It was a pleasing thought that the tools were going *en bloc* from one craftsman to another. Ever since that day, any tools we think may be useful to Richard we hold back until he has seen them.

Richard was a steady buyer of pieces of furniture known in the trade as 'breakers' – furniture whose value lies in its scrap content. Chests of drawers, sideboards, wardrobes and the like he carefully dismantled and stacked according to the type of wood, its grain, figuring and colour. Knobs, handles, castors, locks and other fittings were tied together in sets and hung from the beams. The piles of wood stood head high at the back of the workshop in a happy jumble.

As the years passed his available workspace grew smaller. Before beginning a repair he would search for hours to find a suitable piece with matching grain and colour. He was a slow, meticulous worker of great skill who insisted on mixing his own stains and polishes. Over the years he did much repair work for us. Often a piece would be with him for months on end, which was quite frustrating, but a sympathetic repair is always worth waiting for.

They were a devoted couple; Gwen would tuck little Caroline in her cot and sit on Richard's bench watching him work. She kept the little pot-bellied stove in the corner fed and tended the glue pot. They made a good team and, having great skills, were bound to succeed.

We had bought, at auction, a superb little Georgian oak bureau, country-made but of really good workmanship. It had all its original brass furnishings and, when cleaned of the grime and discoloured polish of a quarter of a century, it revealed itself a rich honey colour which delighted the eye. Sadly it had not been treated with the respect it deserved, for the fall had been allowed to drop without the support of the lopers, dragging the screws of the hinges from the carcass and splitting the wood. One bracket foot was missing completely. A practical man, someone with no poetry in his soul, had nailed a piece of pine in its place. It was a real sleeper. A piece with good potential, it warranted expert repair. We heaved it into the van and took it along to the Radfords, for Arthur was getting more and more reluctant to do repair work.

Richard ran his hands over it, he opened and closed the drawers, appreciating their fit and run after 200 years of use. Looking into the interior he soon found the two secret drawers, as indeed had we. He looked at the bureau for a long time.

Leaning back on his bench, he lit his pipe and folded his arms. He was not a man to be hurried.

'It's a bonny one,' he said after a full minute had gone by. 'It's all quarter-sawn oak.' It was a point I had missed. All the exposed wood – the fall, the drawer fronts, the top and the sides – showed a wealth of medullary rays, that comes only from quarter-sawing of the log. A more expensive and wasteful way than 'run of the mill' sawing, it produces planks that are narrower but with good figuring in them. Another minute passed.

'Well,' I ventured, 'what's it to be?'

'All you dealers think about is money,' he chided. He picked up a piece of wood and chalked a price on it. He turned towards me and smiled. 'Does that frighten you to death?'

It did not. I repressed the question I was bursting to ask, 'When?' I wanted this prestige piece in our shop as soon as possible but we had found that Richard worked best to his own timetable and had a tendency to react adversely if hurried. When the shop is looking a little empty and we have two or three pieces of furniture at Richard's workshop, the temptation is to pick up the telephone and hurry him along. We have always avoided this and over the years it has proved the best policy.

Once we had taken him a set of high-quality rosewood dining chairs. They had the type of breaks along the short grain of the cresting rails which make all cabinet makers wince. He had hung them on the old harness hooks at the back of his workshop, and there they had gathered dust for three months before we tentatively enquired about them. He had gone quiet for a long time, drawing heavily on his pipe before replying, 'I keep looking at them.'

We had known what he meant and had left the matter alone. Little bits of rosewood which matched the grain and colour of the areas of damage had kept appearing on the dust-laden seats of the chairs. Although nothing had actually been done to them, they were in fact being 'worked on'.

A few days after we had taken round the bureau we had a telephone call from Gwen. Would we call in when we were passing?

Richard was putting some pine planks through the planer for a local joiner. He threw the last one contemptuously on to the joiner's trailer. 'Hen hut wood,' he called it, as he searched through his pockets for his pipe. The little bureau still stood on its makeshift foot although the fall had been refitted. His pipe alight, Richard seated himself on the bench. 'You know the secret drawers? Well, take out that one on the right and have a look behind it.'

I did as I was told and peered into the cavity. There was a small loop of tape my finger could not reach. Richard passed me a bent piece of wire and I hooked out another little drawer, hardly an inch in depth. In it was a carefully folded piece of paper containing two bright sovereigns.

'Makes it a cheap bureau,' smiled Richard as I smoothed out the paper and read the thin copperplate writing: 'One for Beatrice and one for Caroline.' I took one sovereign and held it out to Richard.

'No, I don't want it, they're yours,' he said. 'It's not for you, it's for Caroline,' I replied. 'Put it in her shoe when she gets wed.'

Chapter 7

Baz bobbed about the attic, thrusting his penknife into the beams.

'Them's sound enough,' he announced, squatting on an upturned chesford.

I sat on the floor, breaking up bits of plaster and throwing them idly at the candle.

The attic had been floored out to serve as an extra bedroom, probably to accommodate the Irish labourers who had flocked into the dale at haytime in the years before the war. A small window looked out over the common. What a super playroom it would make for the children.

Baz rose from his perch and tapped the underside of the roof. 'It'll want relatting and felting, but nearly all them slates'll turn.'

We clomped down the steps and surveyed the roof, first from the yard and then from the village green. 'We'll need some new ridgestones and a couple of water tables. I'll go see Billy Potts and borrow some scaffolding.' Baz sloped off across the green to The Ship.

Contrary to our friend Colin's confident original forecast, the property in Leeds had taken some time to sell. Until we had the fat cheque from the solicitors in our hand and the shop making money, we had not been able to begin major work on the house. We had picked and piked at the odd job, done a little estimating and a lot of worrying.

Midsummer's day saw the house cradled in scaffolding and as the children ran into the orchard to bring Elspeth the goat in for her morning milking, Baz prised the first ridgestone off the roof. As the sun dropped behind the fell we stretched our aching backs and stared at the slates ranked the length of the scaffolding. Baz rubbed his unshaven chin. 'Five to six ton there.'

The following day, on his instructions, I stripped off the laths and brushed 200 years of dust and cobwebs from the beams and rafters, before creosoting them. That evening Baz began to sort through the slates, rejecting cracked and flaking ones. I shuddered every time a reject crashed into the yard – replacements were expensive and hard to find. The wallplates had rotted away, so we jacked up the rafters and slotted in new ones.

The arrival of the new laths and felt acted like a signal to the gods, for the heavens opened and it rained solidly for a fortnight. We sat in the caravan with the rain lashing on the roof, staring out at the dripping scaffolding. Ted loaned us two stack covers which we lashed over the roof, but no matter how we adjusted them rain always found a way through. The ceilings were lath and plaster and, as they sagged and discoloured under the drenching they received, it became painfully obvious that they would have to be replaced. Another thing we hadn't budgeted for.

Baz discovered a supply of slates on a derelict barn, so we

stripped these off in the rain, hauled them through two muddy fields in the van and stacked them in the yard to be sized and graded. We had moved everything under the shelter of the Dutch barn. Baz sorted, measured and ranked the slates according to size and thickness, and I creosoted all the laths ready for an uptake in the weather. 'Now for the easy bits,' he said as he brought his stone-saw and sawed up slabs of stone to the required thickness to replace the missing water tables. If there was a short period without rain we splodged through the yard and carried the new slates and laths up on to the scaffolding. It was a precarious job, for soon the ladders and planking were coated in mud. With all the preparatory work done, there was nothing we could do but wait for the weather to break.

It was on one of these rain-soaked evenings, as we clustered round the coke stove in the caravan, that Baz appeared with a kitten. The children were thrilled with it, but we were less so ourselves. 'It'll want a good name because it comes from the finest stock in the land,' he joked.

For the rest of the night we racked our brains for a good name for the little ginger tom. When Vicky tucked the two arguing children in their bunks she made the decision for us. 'We'll just call it "the most beautiful cat in the world".' The children pulled the bedclothes up to their chins and smiled their approval.

Although it was a large caravan, two adults, two children, two dogs and a kitten stretched it to its limits. There seemed to be an endless supply of clothes drying round the little stove. We made the decision to keep the dogs outside and I knocked together a run and kennel which, when filled with straw, the dogs seemed to appreciate, for they soon accepted their new confinement.

Mud was a problem. No matter how hard we tried, it carried into the caravan. The whole interior had a dampness about it – clothes, bedding, everything. We would pile the stove high with coke and, placing an old hair dryer under it, blow it up till it glowed red hot. By opening the tiny louvred windows at each end of the caravan, we could dry it out reasonably well.

At last the rain came to an end and we awoke one morning to bright sunshine. A light, westerly wind ruffled the sheets on the roof, and by evening the yard had almost dried out. Baz appeared on time and started to felt and lath the roof. We worked late that night. All the lights were on in the village and the pub car-park was full when we climbed down the ladders and threw our hammers into the barn.

The one luxury I had allowed myself in the cramped caravan was a leather armchair, and I sank into it with aching arms as Baz made off for The Ship. Nothing seemed to tire him. He had worked all day, first drystone walling then felting and latting a large farmhouse roof in the evening, yet he would be in the taproom with pint and dominoes until long after closing time.

Originally the slates had been hung with oak pegs over the laths, but on Baz's advice we nailed them with large-headed galvanized nails, allowing each slate a little movement. 'Let 'em shuffle their arses a bit,' he explained. Every evening now saw the slates creeping higher up the roof, and within a fortnight the ridge tiles were dropped on their bed of cement and the water tables relaid. I cleaned and bitumined the cast-iron gutters before I took down the scaffolding. Come what may in the way of weather, we had a watertight house and could begin its renovation in earnest.

We started at the top, knocking out the lath and plaster

ceilings and, with handkerchiefs tied over our noses and mouths, we chipped plaster from the walls. Plastic fertilizer sacks are invaluable to the house renovator; we filled them with rubble and took vanload after vanload to the tip. Vicky and I, with the children and Baz, could chip the plaster off a room in a night.

The problem now in the caravan wasn't the mud but a covering of white dust on everything, even the dogs. On still evenings, with the windows open, it plumed out over the village green like smoke. Old Mr Hall tottered along from the shop in his slippers. 'Are you on fire?' he asked anxiously.

With the walls clear of lime and the ceilings down, the house was swept through. It was the turning point. The rotten staircase was pulled out and burned; now at last we were ready for building back. We got Richard Radford to make us an exact replica of the staircase in piranha pine, but before this could be fitted we had to have contractors in to injection damp-proof the house.

Baz and I lifted the lozenge-shaped stone flags in the hallway and relaid them on a damp-proof membrane. I found that, including Sundays, I could spend three full days a week on the house. Baz would set me a work schedule and I would struggle to keep to it, for he was a hard taskmaster. Sockets had to be let into the wall and wires run before the plastering could begin. The original plan was to be in the house by Christmas, but this now seemed unlikely. Everything was far more time-consuming and costly than we had estimated. With this in mind, we decided to contract out the plumbing.

Baz's grapevine went into operation once more, resulting in Pete and Dave appearing one day in a van festooned with copper and plastic piping. We had decided on part central heating, run from a high-efficiency back boiler which was fitted with some difficulty into the back of the range.

Vicky and I went off to Northallerton to pick out the bath-room suite and sink units, and to write a cheque which made the biggest hole to date in our budget. The two plumbers were from up the dale and were grand chaps to work with. They sang constantly and made interminable cups of tea, but I had never seen two harder workers. Both were first-class clay pigeon shots and represented the county. Within a week we had an inside toilet and running water, and could enjoy the luxury of a real bath. Lying there soaking after a hard day's work, I could look through the open rafters to our new, sound roof.

Renovating a house is hard work, but some jobs are more pleasurable than others. I had enjoyed the reroofing immensely; it had been backbreaking work but every slate humped across the scaffold to Baz had meant another two square feet of weather-proof house. The worst job had been stripping the old plaster from the walls and bringing down the ceilings.

With the house replumbed and new electrical wiring clipped to the walls and new junction boxes sunk into them, we were ready for replastering. We decided to stain and varnish the staircase and to protect it we tacked a square piece of ply-wood on to each tread. Now we began the laborious job of nailing up plasterboard to renew the ceilings. It was arm-aching work. Baz knocked together a simple frame, almost the height of the room; we would offer up a huge sheet of plas-terboard and jack the frame up on wedges until it trapped one end. I stood on a small stool holding up the middle of the board, while Baz nailed it. My arms would begin to ache. 'Come on, Baz, I'm dropping it.' He would grab a length of wood and jam it under the board. 'Weak buggers, you antiquey men.' The joints were taped and we were ready for the plastering.

Nothing transforms a house so quickly as plastering out. All the wires and pipes are hidden and the walls, gaining some semblance of squareness, make the rooms look liveable in at last. Baz enlisted a friend to help him plaster while Vicky and I mixed for them. I made a simple mixer by clamping an old washing machine motor to a wood frame and soon got the knack of getting the plaster to the right creamy consistency. It was early September and the nights were beginning to draw in, so we rigged up temporary lights from the shop. Every day we lit a fire and turned on the central heating to dry out the rooms.

The problem now was the windows. We had set our hearts on having identical replacements made, but these proved too costly as the glazing bars were finger thin. We had to compromise and order mock sash windows. The best quote we could get was for four months' delivery; this meant we could not be in by Christmas.

Conscious that the warm weather could not last for ever, we decided to turn our attention once more to the exterior. The east elevation of the house had been rendered and this was in a bad state of repair. We found, to our consternation, that we needed planning permission to have this removed. I chipped off a square yard, raked back the joints and repointed them to show the planners how it would look. We did get permission, and started the laborious process of taking off all the render. In some areas a blow of the hammer would dislodge two or three square feet at a time, while in other areas we had to chip away painstakingly at every single square inch. The scaffolding had been returned so, once above head height, we had to work from ladders. It was a very tiring and boring job. The freshly exposed stone was a lighter colour than the rest of the house, but it still looked better than the patchy render. We stapled sheets of polythene over the old rotten window frames to keep the weather out until the replacements were ready.

During this time the garden had suffered. If the shop was quiet Vicky would go out and wage battle on the weeds. The vegetable garden had done well. The load of muck from Ted, coupled with the dark friable soil and frequent waterings, had given us bumper crops, but we had planted without much thought. We did not yet have a deep freeze so the wealth of peas and beans we were growing was an embarrassment; we should really have had more onions and potatoes, which would have kept better.

Anyhow, it was a joy to eat our own produce. The hens kept laying well and the goat was in the full flush of milk. We had decided against letting the goat kid naturally and had the vet inject her to bring on a lactation. She produced far more milk than we needed for the house. The dogs, hens and cat benefited in turn from this excess. Milking her was never a chore. I would fill the little manger with hay, turnip and a handful of dairy nuts and she would stand on a little platform chomping away while I coaxed the milk from her warm udder. She had become quite tame and manageable. The dogs soon learned to respect her, for one butt of her head could send them rolling across the yard. She spent the day tethered in the orchard, where she cropped the apple trees as high as she could reach. In the evenings, after she had been fed and milked, we gave her the freedom of the yard. She would wander in and out of the house at will, a practice we would have to put a stop to because, although it was impossible to move into the house for Christmas, we had decided to at least make the kitchen habitable.

The kitchen floor was quarry-tiled, the ceiling and the walls emulsioned a pale primrose. Night after night in the caravan, Vicky and I drew innumerable plans for it; finally we decided to furnish it wholly with stripped pine. It wasn't the most practical solution but at least it was farmhousy and relatively cheap. As autumn set in we spent more and more time in the kitchen; we were virtually living in there and sleeping in the caravan. It was good to sit at a normal table in a normal chair.

I temporarily glazed the kitchen windows using old picture glass and horticultural glass, roughly puttying them in knowing that at best it could be some weeks before the new frames would replace them. We set about making the kitchen as warm and comfortable as we could. Bunches of mint, sage and parsley hung drying on the beams, and hooky rugs covered the new quarry tiles. We hung an old hammer shotgun over the fireplace and bought two broad-arm Windsor chairs. We decided that this was a room to be lived in, so we let the dogs back in. They formed an uneasy truce with the cat and each soon sorted out its favourite place.

For the first time in months we were warm and comfortable. We had lifted the potatoes and onions and these stood in sacks in the corner. Some evenings it took all our willpower to drag ourselves away from the warm fire to the caravan, which now seemed more cramped than ever. A solemn promise was made that when the house was ready to live in we would drag the caravan up the field and burn it.

Baz still appeared most evenings to carry on with the pointing. Although the nights were drawing in we could still manage to do two or three square yards. I would mix just enough cement before Baz appeared, and when it was done I would flatly refuse to mix any more. Baz would slope off to The Ship and the warm kitchen would claim me. Baz was good to work with; he was even-tempered and surprisingly gentle for such a big strong man. When we were pointing I saw him offer up a trowel of mortar to a joint and withdraw it when he saw a spider scuttling to its doom. A torn bit of cigarette packet fished it out to safety.

'Come on out, you little bugger, tha's as much right to live as I have.'

Chapter 8

There are, in fact, many dealers with considerable wealth behind them who come in at the top of the tree. A few of them will have 'done their homework' and will have gained sufficient knowledge to enable them to become established, but the majority will be lacking in even the rudiments of the trade and these, like the Barracloughs, will soon fall by the wayside.

The trade, particularly when things are buoyant, will support a fair percentage of floating dealers. Their average lifespan is approximately two years, but some singe their wings within a few brief months and disappear, only to be recalled at some idle moment in the saleroom.

'Do you remember that chap with the beard? Bought that wrong dresser.'

Colin Vernon found his way into the antiques trade after a series of small business ventures, all of which managed to feed him but little more. He had been a car dealer, café owner, landscape gardener and run a mobile hot-dog stall. Recently divorced and living in a rented flat, he found himself with a sizeable amount of capital after selling his house and settling up with his ex-wife. Driving along a country lane with nothing much to do, he had been attracted to a farm sale. He'd ended up buying several boxes of blackened cutlery and, on taking them back to his flat and cleaning them up, he had found that the majority were Georgian silver. Colin had a sharp and inquisitive nature and, having hawked this cutlery round several antique shops, quickly formed the opinion that this could be a trade where there were easy pickings. He became a runner. He was a basically lazy but affable fellow, and never lost for a word.

It was a period when trade was good. He decided to specialize in silver and quickly acquired a working knowledge. He spent his time scouring the country antique shops and auction rooms, and soon made connections among the up-market trade in Harrogate and York.

In the early years he did quite well, and this was reflected in his flashy dressing and even flashier cars. A real ladies' man, he changed his girlfriends as often as he changed his linen. This appeared to be about every three months. His girls were all the same tarty type which led Vicky to remark, quite cattily, that if he'd bought a series of wigs he could have stuck with the original girl. He used to call on us quite frequently and was always welcome. He was a hard bargainer but he always paid cash on the nail, an endearing feature in any dealer. Never in a hurry, he would seat himself in a comfortable chair and regale us with stories of his wonderful deals: the George III silver he had bought in a fleamarket that was now at the Grosvenor House Fair; the vast collection of family heirlooms he was buying piece by piece from an impoverished aristocrat. These stories were punctuated with frequent requests to his latest girlfriend to confirm the facts. Being of a generous nature, we agreed that we could believe a quarter of what he said. His stories were always interesting and amusing and he was easy to get on with.

Eventually he married the tartiest of the tarty girlfriends and rented a small shop in the suburbs of York. His stock was small but of good quality. He seemed to be doing very well at first, but as the months passed it became apparent that something was very wrong. His stories became wilder. Calling on him became an embarrassment and, as his stock shrank, his stories grew. The smartness had gone out of his dressing and his aversion to soap became even greater.

Stopping outside his shop one day, we thought he had shut down. It looked empty, but the sign on the door said 'open'. The shop was bare, all the shelves empty, a solitary Doulton character jug stood on the counter. Colin appeared and hurried down the steps to answer the doorbell. His face dropped when he saw us, but quickly brightened.

'I've just been cleaned out by a Yank,' he said.

I congratulated him on his good fortune and wondered why the American hadn't taken the solitary Doulton jug. We were invited into their little back kitchen for coffee. His wife barely acknowledged our greeting, as she rose grudgingly to put the kettle on and rinse three none-too-clean mugs under the tap. Colin sat on the table, clutching his mug in both hands and swinging his legs. He was soon into his familiar routine. Turning to his wife from time to time to request confirmation, story after story poured from him, of great deals and smart buys. Each time she ignored him and kept on filing her nails.

He could tell a good tale and the kitchen was warm on that

cold February morning. Soon the hands of the clock were climbing to midday, so we rose and thanked him for the coffee. We thanked his churlish wife but got no response. He followed us out of the kitchen, still chatting away optimistically.

I had my hand on the door handle when he called back to his wife, 'Shall we have some fish and chips for lunch?'

Back came the angry shout, 'You know we can't afford bloody fish and chips.'

For the first time I saw Colin look really crestfallen. Just cleaned out by an American, only one item left in the shop and yet he couldn't afford fish and chips. I turned back and picked up the Doulton jug.

'What's this got to be, Colin?' I said. 'It's a nice jug.'

His face brightened; he slipped easily into his salesman guise. He was asking far too much for the jug but we paid his asking price. At least now they would be able to afford fish and chips for lunch.

It was sad to see him in this state. With him the harsher reality became the more he fantasized. The next time we passed the shop it was closed and empty. We learned later on the grapevine that his wife had left him and he'd moved to the south coast, to work in an amusement arcade – no doubt still full of dreams and chasing tarty birds.

The aristocracy of the trade is formed from a very small group of antique dealers. They are usually second-, third- or even fourth-generation dealers. Not only must working capital and knowledge be handed on, but also a love of the trade. Furthermore, a family business which has endured for eighty years or more must undoubtedly have gone through periods when greater returns could have been had by investing time and capital elsewhere. When times are bad the big family firms go on buying; it is the lesser dealers who have to pull in their horns and weather the storm. The old adage, 'buy when times are bad and sell when times are good', is truer in this trade than most.

With a long-established family firm, the aura of discretion and respectability is all-important. Whether buying or selling, the relationship between dealer and client is handled as professionally as that between doctor and patient. If the client is selling, the dealer's Volvo will glide into his drive at dusk. A minimum of gentlemanly haggling over a leisurely glass or two of port and the goods are loaded under the cover of darkness, safe from the eyes of prying neighbours.

Once the goods are in the dealer's shop, wild horses couldn't drag the name of the vendor from him. He has to protect his source. He may hint that they are from a titled family or from the collection of a noted connoisseur, but the naming of names is taboo. Many families go through periods when the need is for immediate cash; the causes of these are manifold but drink and gambling come high on the list.

Often the relationship between vendor and dealer starts with a few mediocre pieces offered for sale with a transparent excuse. As confidence grows, more desirable treasures are brought out. It is not unknown for a dealer to buy, over a period of a few years, the entire contents of a house that it might have taken three or four generations to assemble. On his first visit the dealer will buy the mediocre bits, quite often above their true value. He will be the epitome of gentlemanly discretion. Carefully counting out the crisp banknotes from a purposefully fat wallet, he will quietly appraise the furnishings in the room. A request to visit the bathroom will enable him to assess the rest of the house contents as far as he can, but he will do nothing which might jeopardize the new relationship.

Martin was a third-generation antique dealer. He had acquired his extensive knowledge of the trade more by absorption than anything else. Subjected to continual talk of antiques from childhood and surrounded by the better things in life, he had a vast range of interests. He was equally at home with a Russian bronze as with an Impressionist painting or a piece of English oak.

He called on us late one evening in August, as Vicky was closing the shop. He took his time going around the stock, everything coming under his careful scrutiny. Finally he picked the best piece of furniture in the shop, a small rosewood canterbury. We had gone over the top when we bought it, but it was such a fine little piece, of good colour and proportions, and both Vicky and I have a love of rosewood.

'What can you do that for?' he asked pleasantly.

We have a simple code on the back of each price ticket: if you place your fingers over the two end digits, the ones remaining show the price we have paid for the piece. Vicky knelt by the canterbury, thinking furiously. She knew who he was – Martin de Trafford, a really good contact. She quoted him a price which barely covered us. He didn't haggle, he just wrote out a cheque and, with a curt 'Goodnight', he was off.

The de Traffords live in a large country house some thirty miles away. They are the top dealers in the county. When they walk into a saleroom we of lesser ilk groan inwardly. Martin started calling on us regularly. At first he was polite but cool and businesslike. Gradually we got to know him, and he us. Vicky is a passably good cook but for some unknown reason she makes the worst coffee in Yorkshire. Martin sat on the panel-backed settee toying with his.

'We have some things,' he began, then paused, 'which may interest you. They're stuff we've had to buy but they're not really in our line.' He meant the mediocre stuff.

The fine Georgian house set in four acres of manicured gardens was riddled with alarms and infra-red beams. A pair of unfriendly Dobermann pinschers roamed the grounds at night and each vehicle was automatically photographed as it passed through the imposing gateposts.

I drove the van into the stable yard where Martin was waiting for us. The goods were laid out in the old coach house, decent middle-of-the-road stuff together with a few pieces of unstripped pine. Nothing was priced.

'Well, Martin, what do you want for it?' I asked, picking up an Edwardian cake stand.

'Give me a price for the lot,' he replied.

I don't like doing that with the trade. 'Come on, Martin, I can't be both buyer and seller.'

'Just go over it and make me a cash offer.' He smiled and walked back into the house.

It took Vicky and me almost an hour to price the stuff, which ranged from an Anglo-Indian desk to a glass dome filled with stuffed humming birds. It totalled more than the cash we had with us.

Martin shrugged his shoulders. 'OK, if that's it.' I explained we hadn't enough cash with us to cover it and said I'd put a cheque in the post to cover the discrepancy. 'No! No cheques,' he replied, smiling. 'Give me it some other time.'

It was obvious that the mediocre pieces were sold off, cash, to provide him with what is known in the trade as 'a little back pocket money'.

On our second visit, some weeks later, Martin took us round the house. The rooms used by the family were impeccably furnished; the oil paintings would have graced any top-class London gallery and the *objets d'art*, scattered with studied carelessness, were worth a king's ransom.

Martin's passion was for clocks. In the hall stood his most prized possession, a quarter-striking calendar long-case by Thomas Tompion. Of the type known as 'bolt and shutter maintaining power', it was housed in a gleaming walnut case, its neat face flanked by tapered barley-twist pillars. Over the Adam fireplace a carved *lignum vitae* bracket carried his Nibb bracket clock. Martin explained to us that the Nibb was the real reason for all the security precautions. It was so desirable, so valuable and so portable that the insurance company flatly refused to cover it.

His father had retired from the business but still lived in the house. He spent most of his time in the kitchen, his broad-arm Windsor chair pulled well up to the Aga. We only spoke to him once. Martin had laid out the stuff in the coach house and as usual had left Vicky and me pricing it up.

The old man shuffled across the yard in his carpet slippers and picked his way through the goods towards us. 'You the people from Ramsthwaite?' The bright, almost periwinkle-blue eyes fixed on mine. 'You don't pay much,' he went on.

'We pay what we can, and a bit more sometimes,' I countered.

He gave a little laugh, and tapped a Victorian toilet mirror with his stick. 'How much have you put down for this?'

'Twenty pounds,' I told him.

'That's cheap, that's cheap.'

'Well, times are slow.'

He pottered about the coach house, muttering, 'Times are slow, are they?' Finally he came up to me and fixed me with his bright eyes again. 'I bought a George III wine table for twelve pounds ten shillings in 1926 and sold it in 1928 for fifteen pounds – *that* was slow times, son.'

He turned and hobbled back to his warm kitchen, wreathed in tobacco smoke.

Chapter 9

It was probably our frequent visits to Long John's which sparked off the children's desire to have a pony. As soon as the van pulled into his yard after the steep climb up the track, they would tumble out and go in search of Polly.

The quiet dales mare, almost fifteen years old, was never either tethered or stabled but had the run of the holding. On warm summer days she would graze quite high on the fell, but bad weather would find her under the Dutch barn, her flank pressed against the straw bales. She always adopted the same stance, with her head held well down, favouring her rear offside leg.

The children adored her. She would stand quiet as an old sheep while they patted and stroked her and she gently took offered titbits from their small hands. Long John had worked her regularly when she was younger, carting dung and logs and riding after the sheep on the high fell with nothing more than a folded sack for a saddle. She'd foaled well in her younger years, having been put to a variety of stallions. She was a pure-bred

Dales mare and Long John regretted that he'd never put her to a pedigree stallion and kept the strain.

The idea of having a Dales pony grew on us. Vicky and I discussed it at night when the children were asleep.

'We're thinking of getting a pony,' I told Ted.

He rubbed his nose thoughtfully. 'Trouble wi' horses is, they eat all the time.'

The economics of it were all wrong; if we bought a mare we'd no doubt foal it and the mare could work around the smallholding, but with the high cost of feed she would always be a financial liability. We could keep three or even four sheep in place of a pony. Although the shop was open and making money we were not in a strong financial position but, like the goat, the hens and the newly acquired ducks, a pony fitted into our idealized picture of country life, and we felt it would be good for the children. There are disadvantages as well as advantages to living in the country. Any activities always seem to be far flung and one has to make a real effort to take the children probably ten miles or more to see a friend, or to the swimming baths or pictures. Several of the children in the village had ponies and there were safe bridleways over the common and on to the fell.

Finally we decided we would buy a pony. I followed up several advertisements in a local newspaper, with no success. The children were still only nine and seven, and it was important that we had a quiet pony. One described as 'good to shoe and box' turned out to be a wild-eyed monster, and the 'fourteen hands, ride or drive' had never seen a pair of shafts in its life. Eventually, through some friends, we got in touch with Dr and Mrs Snow, who had a small stud of Dales ponies on their Durham farm. They seemed to have just the animal we were looking for.

I didn't take the children on this expedition, for obvious reasons. One Sunday afternoon towards the end of August, Long John and I set out in the van for Durham.

'What a smashing place,' Long John whispered as we drove into the yard.

Their set-up was impressive: roomy loose-boxes set around three sides of a cobbled yard, a large stone-built hay barn supported a lean-to, under which stood an exercise cart and a beautifully restored four-wheeled dog cart. The Snows had two full-time girl grooms and everything was immaculately kept. Most of the horses were out at grass and only two or three of the boxes were occupied.

Topic was led out into the centre of the yard. She was glistening coal black, with a white blaze and four white feet. About fourteen hands high, well boned with a goodly amount of muscle, she was a really attractive pony. She was clearly also friendly, responding to the petting I gave her. As Long John and I walked around her, she turned her head and watched with an intelligent eye. I knew very little about horses, which was why I had brought Long John along. He examined her ears, eyes and mouth, looked at each leg in turn and asked for her to be walked around the yard. Next, he had the girl groom trot her round the paddock where Topic showed off her nice crisp action. Long John stood back, his arms akimbo, his eyes fixed on the pony.

'She'll do for me, son!'

'She's all right, then?'

'Can't fault her.'

Mrs Snow asked if we would like to see her put to the exercise cart. I was keen on this because any pony we had would see more shaft work than anything else. The Snows used a Cape cart harness, which has a broad breastband instead of the conventional collar. I have never liked this kind of harness; it is all right for mere exercise, but for real pulling one needs a conventional collar to sit on the shoulder bones of the animal. The experts tell us that technically a horse doesn't pull a cart, it pushes it.

I climbed into the exercise cart alongside Mrs Snow, she took up the reins and gave Topic the command to 'walk on'. I was pleased to see that we were going down the drive to the main road and not merely driving around a paddock. She was obviously not frightened to put Topic in traffic. The pony was walked for about a quarter of a mile; she pricked her ears and lifted her head a little at the passing traffic but was quite steady. As we came to a straight, clear piece of road, Mrs Snow slapped the reins and commanded the pony to 'trot on'. Topic had a brisk and easy action.

We did a good two miles before returning to the yard. Long John stroked her flanks to see how much sweat she had raised, and we both noticed that the brisk trot had hardly affected her breathing. They said she was guaranteed sound in both wind and limb, and sound in wind and limb she seemed to be.

Mrs Snow brought tea out on to the lawn and as we sat around the little wrought-iron table in the late summer sunshine the talk was all of horses. The Snows were delighted to talk to someone who had actually worked a smallholding with Dales ponies, and Long John warmed to the task. He had made a real effort that morning, having shaved and put on a clean pair of jeans and a sweater with no more than two holes in it. He told of Polly carrying him and two bales of hay on to the high fell in deep winter, and how steady and quiet and understanding she had been when he pulled out a bogged-down cow with her. He told of bringing the first-born lambs of spring back to the holding in panniers across her back, and of every-day work around the holding.

The Snows were fascinated. Their questions came thick and fast. 'What's jagging?' 'How near to foaling did you work her?' 'Doesn't the scree cut her frogs?' Although they were leading breeders and they had been associated with Dales ponies for years, they had never had the occasion to work one. All their stock was kept fit and built up muscle either on the lungeing rein or in the exercise cart. The sociologists who measure, categorize and pigeonhole everyone according to their position on the socio-economic scale would have put the Snows and Long John poles apart, but they got on like a house on fire. Their common ground was a basic honesty and a deep love of the Dales pony. Long John had shown them the ultimate respect; all afternoon not one obscenity had passed his lips.

The Snows tactfully retired, leaving Long John and me with a second cup of tea to discuss the pony. They were asking a high price for her but Long John again said he couldn't fault the animal. I had fallen in love with her at first sight. I could not remember all the old adage about ponies with white socks but I could remember the bit that went:

Three white socks try it,
Four white socks buy it.

I looked at Long John. 'Well, what shall I do?'

He eased his lanky frame into the little garden chair. 'Well, it's your money, son, but if you want to buy the best, there it is.'

We went into the kitchen and I wrote out the cheque and arranged to come for her the following Sunday.

We drove home in high spirits, talking of nothing but ponies, gears and carts. When I got back to the caravan the children were sat having their tea. They questioned me eagerly as to where I'd been. I winked at Vicky. 'I've been to see a man about a dog.'

'You've been to look at a pony!' they shouted together. 'Did you buy it?'

Long John let the cat out of the bag. 'We are fetching her next Sunday.'

Vicky went into the lean-to and got cracking with bacon and eggs for two hungry horse-buyers, as I sat and described Topic to two excited children.

The following Sunday I borrowed a single horse trailer from Mr and Mrs Martin, we bundled the children and dogs into the van and set off for the Snows' farm. The children had raided the dairy and their pockets were stuffed with carrots and apples. As we pulled into the yard the Snows were waiting to greet us, and Topic was brought from her box to be met with oohs and ahs of approval. The carrots and apples were readily accepted and, after the petting and stroking were over, I walked her around the yard and up the ramp into the box. On my previous visit I had noticed that the Snows had one or two good antiques in their house, so with half an eye on business I gave them a card and cordially invited them to call in and see Topic any time they were passing.

We have had Topic for five years now. She has carried Vicky and the children over the fell on picnics, worked honestly round the holding and given us two grand foals. The Snows have called to see us several times since we bought Topic, and I managed to sell them a nice brass-faced longcase clock by Snow of Pateley Bridge. The good Doctor had started to haggle over the

97

price of it, but I had remembered his own words when we had gone to buy Topic.

'You can't get quality on the cheap.' He just smiled and pulled out his cheque book.

Several of the villagers came round to see Topic when she arrived. Old Mr Hall stroked her fat rump and felt down her legs.

'Just as they should be,' he said with approval.

'Have you worked with horses?' I asked him.

'Worked wi' horses? Spent me life with 'em.' He fussed around Topic and told us of his years as a carter, until his daughter called from the village green.

'Come on, yer dinner's on the table.'

The old man turned at the bottom of the yard, a twinkle in his eye. 'It's not proper, in front of your lady wife. When I come back, remind me to tell thee about a carter's rights.'

Every Sunday evening, rain or shine, Vicky and I took the children and dogs the one-and-a-half-mile length of Drover's Lane. The lane was wide, a good twenty paces wide, but the elder and blackthorn had colonized its bankings and in some places the bushes nearly touched. A single-track footpath wound down its length, and where the bushes had not taken over each little island of grass carried a wealth of wild flowers.

To the south of the lane lay the huge pastures of the Estate, but on the north side the land was divided into small garths of no more than two or three acres each. Almost every garth had its small stone barn, for before the turn of the century nearly every cottage had its parcel of land to support the house cow, or keep a trap pony. The beck runs along the south of the lane, on Estate land. At intervals it has been tapped into the lane to feed stone-lined sinks where the cottager could fill his bucket.

Over the years the garths have been bought up by a handful of farmers and the dividing walls breached to make more economically worked pieces of land. One garth remained untouched, its walls and barn intact, its waist-high brown grass showing it was neither grazed nor cut. It belonged to Nellie May. She would not sell it and she would not rent it.

Nellie May lived in a tiny cottage at the bottom of the common. She and her husband had moved there twenty years ago when they had given up the travelling life. Her husband had bought the garth because he did a little horse dealing, 'to keep his hand in', as he said. Since his death five years ago, nothing had been done with the garth. Thistles, nettles and ground elder had taken over and the land was riddled with moles.

We had had hardly any contact with the old woman. She kept herself very much to herself and was at odds with most of the villagers, but Ted visited her at least once a week, taking her a few eggs and occasionally a sack of logs. He and her late husband had been good friends. We asked Ted to approach her and see if she would rent us the land. Not holding out much hope, we were surprised when Ted called in one evening and said that Nellie May wanted to see us.

'Both of you, mind, she wants to see both of you,' he added.

We both went round to the little cottage the following morning. Nellie May opened her door and stared at us.

'Ted said you wanted to see us.'

She said nothing but turned back into the cottage, leaving the door open. I looked at Vicky. 'Did she expect us to follow her in?' I knocked at the door and walked in tentatively, Vicky following. Nellie had seated herself by the fire and pulled a shawl around her shoulders.

'Shut the door and sit down,' she commanded. We shut the door and we sat down.

'You want to rent the land?' I thought I would let Vicky answer. Sometimes it is better when a woman talks to a woman.

'Yes,' said Vicky, 'we have got a pony and would like to graze it down there, then we could cut the garth behind the house for hay.' We also had plans for fattening a couple of pigs in the barn but thought best to say nothing of this yet.

The small dark eyes watched us intently, her mouth twitched continually as her hands folded and unfolded in her lap. 'Well! How much?'

We were a bit taken aback. We had expected her to state a price. The night before we had discussed nothing else but the land, and had decided that we would pay no more than £100 a year for it. 'Well,' I began, 'we were thinking of seventy-five pounds a year.'

Nellie May screwed up her face. 'How much is that a week?'

I remembered how Ted had told us she had never got into the way of the 'new money', as she put it. 'That's thirty bob a week,' I said. 'When do you want paying?'

'Bring it every Thursday,' she replied, rising from her chair with difficulty. She walked across to Vicky, stretched out a thin brown hand and touched Vicky's hair. 'I had hair like that when I got wed.' Nellie May held the door open for us. 'Does them hens of yours lay well?'

I took the hint, and every Thursday night I delivered thirty bob and a few eggs to the old woman.

*

They say that if you want bad grass, cut it bad and graze it bad. The garth had been neither cut nor grazed for five years and the tough brown grass and weed stood waist high. We got Ted to cut what he could with his grey Ferguson, and burned off the rest. The hay we made was coarse, brittle stuff and I could see no food value in it. 'Fill-belly for bullocks,' Ted called it.

We forked it into long windrows and rolled them down the hill to the barn. It was hot, sticky work but we all enjoyed it. Vicky brought a picnic hamper and three nights running we had our suppers sat on the brown prickly ground, tired and dusty.

Ted put a top dressing on the land for us, and within a fortnight a light green haze of new grass covered the garth. Another fortnight and Topic was hock-deep in what Ted described as 'fair stuff'.

I hid a hedge slasher at the top of the lane and each time we went to see Topic I slashed back the hedges. Being left-handed, I slashed the left side going down and the right coming back. I soon had the lane wide enough for the little coup cart we had built for the pony. Harness was a problem. New trap harness to fit a fourteen-hands pony is expensive and hardly strong enough for the jobs we had in mind. I managed to get a collar and cart saddle but no breeching could be found anywhere, so I got the retired saddler in Lalbeck to make me one. He came out with his son-in-law to measure Topic. It was the first new piece of harness he had made for thirty years. He pushed his hands between Topic's neck and the collar, heightened the shaft hangers on the saddle and coloured the breeching to match. We had a sound set of working gears for our pony.

We had made the coup cart as near to the old pattern as we could, but we used exterior plywood for the panels and floor to make it as light as possible. Topic soon took to her new task. She was a willing worker and threw her neck into the collar, as she dragged the little cart with its load of children up and down the lane. We wanted her to build up some muscle and check the gears for rubbing and chafing before we gave her a real load to pull. We painted the cart beige and Vicky carefully stencilled our name and address on the near side.

As she stepped back to admire it, I told her I could not wait to exercise my new right as a carter.

'New right?' she enquired.

I had met Mr Hall in the lane and he had kept his promise to tell me about a carter's rights. 'Yes, under English law a carter in charge of a horse is legally entitled to urinate on the highway – as long as he goes to the offside of his vehicle and makes it discreet.'

Chapter 10

Ever since we had outwitted them at the Kebblestones farm sale, the Ring had watched us like hawks. They either bid us out of everything or forced us to pay a price which left us with little or no profit. We tried every subterfuge in the book but to little avail. Along with a couple of other dealers, Fiery Frank was calling regularly and the shipping goods side of the business was taking off. Only a small proportion of our stock was bought privately so we were forced to travel back to the West Riding to buy. They were long, tiring days and our petrol bills were enormous, but we had no alternative.

Out of every vanload we brought north we put approximately half into the local sales. The Ring, so intent on keeping us out, would buy it in at prices which more than covered the commission and expenses. In fact it was quite profitable. If things were flagging I only had to step forward and make a noticeable bid for the Ring to regain interest. Sometimes when we had had a good day I would take the last item to a ridiculous price just to see how far they would go. More often than not we left the auction room with money in our pockets and an empty van.

It was the last week in August. Long John's voice blared down the telephone. 'Aunt Flo has died. Want you to come and look at some stuff.'

Long John's Aunt Flo had lived in a tiny cottage at the head of the dale. A small, frail woman, she had turned a little funny in her last years. Carefully banking her pension, she tried to live on the few hundred pounds a year she got from renting two fields she owned down by the river. Of late, she had started eating rabbits which had been killed on the road and at night scouring the dustbins of the neighbouring hamlet.

I pushed open the door of the cottage. It was dark, damp and musty. The old lady had lived frugally, with little in the way of possessions. The kitchen stank. A small deal table, thick with newspapers, had three odd chairs set around it. Painted in different primary colours, they were the only things to relieve the drabness of the room. The brown salt-glazed sink was filled with dirty pans, each of which had grown a rim of furry mould. The sitting room was sparsely furnished; a couch and a table sat on the bare flagged floor, both were riddled with woodworm. Piles of old newspapers stood in each corner. The chenille cloth covering the table matched the pelmet over the Yorkist range, both were faded mustard and rotten to the touch. Upstairs yielded nothing of value. A plywood bedroom suite, again suffering from the worm, and a small iron bedstead piled with an assortment of blankets and coats. There was not one picture or carpet in the cottage. We apologized to Long John and hurried home, itching for a good wash.

Fatty Batty once defined a marquee as, 'a wood and canvas structure erected by auctioneers in the grounds of a country house in order to double the prices'. Cottage sales are in the same vein as marquee sales. Fatty's witticism put the germ of an idea into my mind. If Long John was agreeable, we would pack some decent furniture into the late Aunt Flo's cottage and have an auction sale.

Long John, no lover of the Ring, was agreeable. In fact he seized on the idea readily and set to work carting the worst of the rubbish to the tip. Vicky mopped the floors with a solution so strong in disinfectant it made our eyes water, while I washed the windows and scrubbed what was left in the sad little kitchen. Long John took a scythe to the long grass around the cottage and set several of his 'troffs', now packed with pansies and primulas, on the wall. By the time the night fell the little cottage was transformed. We left it with the windows wide open, a gentle breeze billowing the raggy curtains into the dark rooms.

For two days we carted furniture up the dale and filled the cottage. Aunt Flo's pathetic belongings were stood in the garden to blow the smell off them and then packed into the outhouse. It was no good filling the place with mediocre bits and pieces, we had to have stuff of sufficient quality to fetch the Ring and draw enough money from their pockets to cover our expenses and show a profit. We decided to leave the best of the smalls packed in tea-chests and to take the very best of the furniture up to the cottage the night before the sale.

Long John was carefully tacking chicken wire over what remained of the garden gate. 'I'll bring me geese up and put 'em in here until the sale. No bugger will get past them.'

The next problem was to find an auctioneer. Long John knew a retired cattle auctioneer who occasionally needed the price of a bottle. I was decidedly unsure when first introduced to Sam. His breath would have felled an elephant, but he had a clear mind and talked sound business.

'Is he square?' I asked Long John.

'Square as any of 'em,' came the reply.

The advertisements were put out: 'The complete house contents of the late Miss Florence Metcalfe', and in much smaller lettering, 'and other vendors' – truthful because the worldly goods of the late Aunt Flo nestling in the outhouse would also be offered for auction.

Sam was adamant. The sale had to be advertised for at least a fortnight prior to it taking place. We had great misgivings – suddenly it did not seem such a good idea. On several nights I drove up to the cottage and walked round the outside of the garden wall, Long John's geese hissing angrily at me.

The night before the sale I took an oak dresser, a grandfather clock and two Windsor chairs up to the cottage. Long John lighted a fire and set his camp bed in front of it. It was drizzling steadily. We needed a fine day for the sale. We stood in the garden staring at the sky. What would tomorrow bring?

'It'll be all right, it'll be fine tomorrow,' Long John assured me. How did he know, astute countryman that he was? Rooks flying high? Fish feeding on the surface of the beck? Dung flies clustering on a southern wall?

'No!' he replied curtly. 'It sez so on the wireless.'

I drove home to a sleepless night.

The morning of the sale I milked the goat and fed the hens early. It was a Saturday and the world was bathed in brilliant sunshine. It was a real Indian summer; the ideal day for a cottage sale. Vicky insisted on coming to the sale with me as we had so much at stake. Gwen Radford came to open the shop for us and she and Vicky chatted while I made doorstop sand-wiches and filled two vacuum flasks.

Long John was hard at work when we arrived. He'd donned a brown smock and, with Sam's steward, had carried most of the furniture into the garden. Three trestle tables had been set up and these were covered with the Staffordshire figures, some good brass and copper and the trivia which is to be found in every household. We'd gathered together a lot of prints and two decent oil paintings. These were arranged against the garden wall, shaded from the sun. There was one thing we had overlooked – over twenty pictures and not one picture rail or hook in the cottage. More of a giveaway, there were none of the lighter patches on the wallpaper which pictures always leave. The slim little cottage clock looked well in its alcove in the sitting room, it gave the impression it had lived there all its life but, once moved, there would be no brighter patch behind to give it provenance.

Sam had agreed to do the auction for a fixed price if we paid for the advertising and the out-of-pocket expenses. His clerk had set up office in the kitchen and was emptying bags of change into the old-fashioned wooden till. Out in the garden, Vicky had set out our sandwiches and flasks on a square of white linen. I could eat nothing, my stomach was full of butterflies.

There was a good turnout, the cottage and garden were thronged with people and the sunlight glinted from the roofs of cars parked the entire length of the track, but as yet there was no sign of the Ring. I had no need to view the sale, for I knew each piece intimately. In the north the smalls are sold first, then the furniture, saving the best piece for last.

It was nearly one o'clock and still no sign of the Ring. Long

John was enjoying himself immensely. His brown smock gave him a certain standing in the proceedings and he answered the many questions put to him with good-natured ease. He was an adroit liar and a false but interesting history was instantly created for every item.

'She brought that back from the Wembley Exhibition of 1921,' he told a woman who was showing interest in a brass tea caddy I'd bought at a fleamarket a fortnight ago.

Wembley Exhibition of 1921 indeed! Poor Aunt Flo had never been out of the dale in her life. A large copper kettle held pride of place on the table of brass and copper items. We'd bought it from Fiery Frank. It was Georgian, with an acorn finial to its lid, and its rosy copper had been polished to a silky sheen. A well-dressed couple lifted it from the table. Long John pounced.

'Me grandad won that in a quoits match before the First World War,' he told them.

I winced and went to find the children. They were in the back of Long John's van. He had brought an assortment of livestock to sell. Housed in a variety of boxes with wire netting crudely tacked across their fronts were the oldest bantam cock I'd ever seen, several rabbits and a pair of gill ferrets. The rabbits were no bigger than a man's fist; pink twitching noses poked through the netting to take the dandelion leaves Sally and Peter offered.

'Can we have a rabbit, Daddy?' they asked.

'No!' I answered abruptly, for I was getting quite irritable. None of the Ring had shown up. It was going to be a fiasco; the auctioneer reeked of whisky and there were glaring mistakes in the make-up of the cottage contents. We had burned all Aunt Flo's linen and soft goods and had brought none to make up the deficiency. A glass-topped showcase filled with jewellery had appeared on one of the tables. I had no idea where it had come from. I lay down beside Vicky. The sky was a cloudless bowl of blue, martins wheeled and shrieked overhead and the grass, crushed by hundreds of feet, smelled sweet. Lazy bees droned in and out of the foxgloves and a cat stretched idly and licked itself on the tin roof of the outbuilding.

At last it was one o'clock. The clerk carried a box into the centre of the garden and Sam, with a heavy hand on the clerk's shoulder, heaved himself on to it. He looked none too steady.

'We are shelling today on behalf of the executors of the late Miss Metcalf,' he belched and added quietly, 'and other vendors.' He started reading out the conditions of sale but soon tired of it, handing the sheet to his clerk. 'You know them as well as I do. Let's make a start. Lot one, Ladies and Gentlemen.'

Long John held up a tray of glassware. 'There's some good stuff on here, Sam.'

It fetched eight pounds – a good price.

Tray followed tray, every one bringing a favourable comment from Long John. The bidding was brisk and Sam kept the crowd in a good mood. I watched him closely. He was a good auctioneer. He never missed a bid and had a constant easy flow of repartee which jollied things along. I warmed towards him. Vicky sat on a tree stump with calculator and pad, noting every price, for although Lohn John had vouched for Sam we had a distrust of all auctioneers. The brass and copper fetched high prices. The wealthy-looking couple got the Georgian kettle at a price just short of twice what I had paid Fiery Frank for it. No doubt its recently acquired history will stick to it for the rest of its days. It turned out that the showcase full of jewellery

109

belonged to Sam, and he took an appreciable time to sell it. There were some good pieces and Sam milked every one.

Next came the pictures. The prints were poor, foxed and stained Victorian scenes of cattle knee-deep in water and a scattering of religious subjects. We barely cleared ourselves. The first oil on canvas to be offered was a river scene. It was nothing special, a competent little picture signed with a mono-gram and badly in need of cleaning.

'I have several proxy bids on this painting and must start it at £100,' Sam announced, looking around. He paused, his cane hovering above a fat palm. 'I shall sell it,' he threatened, 'I shall sell it on the maiden bid.' Again a pause. He raised his cane to shoulder height.

'And ten,' came a voice from the back of the crowd. I recognized it immediately: it was Elly. They were here. I looked across at Vicky and smiled. She too had recognized the voice.

'One-twenty here,' said Sam, stabbing at his chest with the cane.

'One-thirty,' replied Elly.

The bidding went on until the cane finally came down at £170.

'Mr Ellwood, I believe,' smiled Sam.

The second oil, a harvest scene on board, did even better. I thought it was Continental but Sam confidently described it as English school, nineteenth century. It was unsigned but defi-nitely the better of the two paintings. A modest start at fifty pounds had a more satisfactory conclusion. '£220, same buyer,' beamed Sam.

We were well into profit on the two oils. Elly was obviously buying for the Ring today and I was itching to get in on the bidding.

Sam dropped heavily from his box and waved to his clerk to take it across to where Aunt Flo's pathetic belongings were stacked. He knew his job. He wanted to sell the junk while he still had a good crowd and things were buoyant. He made a detour to the kitchen window, where Long John handed him a pint pot. Sam gulped down its contents and was still wiping his fat jowls with a large spotted handkerchief as he remounted the box.

Long John disentangled the iron bed-ends from the pile and leaned them together. Sam waved his cane at them. 'Thish shtuff ish comin' into itsh own, a bit o' shandpaper an' paint an' themsh bijou.' The crowd laughed. 'Down London them 'ud fetch £100 – give us a quid.'

The bed-ends went to a laughing young couple for fifteen pounds. Sam grinned at the pretty wife as she half hid behind her husband, her body shaking with laughter. 'Bijou them, luv – bijou.' He was obviously taken with the word. He shuffled his feet on the box to make a right-angled turn to where Long John sorted the pile. 'Any more bijou in there, John?'

It was obvious that Aunt Flo's belongings were going to be milked for every penny, so I gathered the children and challenged them to a race down to the river. As they eagerly climbed the wall I grabbed Long John's elbow. 'Isn't he getting a bit –?' I trembled a hand in front of my mouth to indicate drinking.

A grin spread across his hairy face as he lifted up a tattered bedroom chair. 'He's puttin' it on a bit. Have confidence, my boy, this bugger can plait sawdust.'

Chapter 11

We dangled our hot feet in the icy water. The river ran swiftly here over a bed of smooth cobbles, pale beige eggstones shimmering through the brown water.

It was going to be a long hard day, but it was good to get away from the house and shop and to be with the children. I don't know who started the playful splashing, but all three of us were soaking wet when we ran panting up the field in answer to Vicky's frantic waving. Sam was starting on our furniture.

A panelled kist with a replacement bottom was knocked down to a private buyer for £250. The new bottom boards had been papered over with an 1875 *Newcastle Chronicle*. Its yellowed pages must have been highly valued by our happy friend, because he had paid well over the odds for the kist.

All the furniture was expensive. Sam started everything off at a low price. There is a lot of psychology and a bit of theatre in auctioneering. A dealer will fix a break-off price in his mind and stick to it, but some private buyers, once they are caught up in the bidding, let the desire to possess overcome all else. There are always a few sore heads the morning after an auction. Sometimes rival dealers will lock horns over a desirable piece, and any new dealer appearing on the circuit always has to have his nose bloodied. Then there is gravy to be had.

There were no new faces here today, but there was a good show of private buyers and the Ring was strong. Two Windsor chairs with cow-horn stretchers were offered by Sam as a pair. A mistake, I thought, as there were glaring differences in the turning of the legs. I changed my mind when they fetched £350 – good old Elly again.

Vicky was quite excited; another couple of hundred pounds and we were in the clear, with the best items of furniture still to come. Sam sweated on his box. He doffed his coat and handed it to Long John in exchange for another pint pot. The large spotted handkerchief came out again. It swept under the fat chops and described a graceful arc to be stuffed back into the waistcoat pocket. He was getting more and more voluble.

Long John was not to be outdone. Whatever nectar appeared in those pint pots, Long John had had his share. His repeated comment, 'This is a good 'un,' was applied to everything, good and bad alike. Sam took the furniture slowly, for he had got to that stage of inebriation where a man realizes that he is going to have to be careful if he is to get through the day. His grin never failed, but his speech became slow and measured.

I had bought a good clean dresser some weeks previously and had paid quite a lot of money for it. This was the lot I'd decided to take on the Ring with. Elly was buying in and the rest of the gang crowded round Fatty's Mercedes. They were in high spirits. Sam had had to ask them to be quiet more than once. We had no common ground with the lads of the Ring but we were on nodding terms with them, and I went up to the little group to pass the time of day, more to make my presence known than anything else.

There was a lot of interest in the dresser. A nice clean honest one with a good patina, well proportioned and with all its original handles, it was a desirable piece. It was the star of the sale and Sam realized it. He ordered the crowd back and had his box moved in front of it. The clerk's shoulder dipped dutifully as he dragged his fat body up on to the makeshift rostrum. He was perspiring freely as he began a paean of praise which excelled everything he had done before.

It was without a doubt the finest piece of furniture ever to come before him. It was original, untouched and desirable. 'Such pieces are not often come by,' he told the crowd. 'You can go many a long day and not find a dresser like this.' Finally he added seriously, 'This dresser should not go out of the dale.'

I failed to see why, because I had only brought it into the dale the week before.

Long John stood in the doorway of the outhouse. I pushed past him into the cool interior, taking care to see that the Ring noticed me.

'More bids on the book,' shouted Sam. 'I'll have to start it at £500.'

I was glad to be out of the hot sun. My palms were sweaty and I felt quite sick. I had paid a lot of money for the dresser; it was our biggest gamble. It had stood out all day in the hot sun and I was worried about the patina, but it did not seem to have been adversely affected. Sam opened the bidding at £500. It climbed slowly, in twenty-pound bids, to £800. It was still less than I had paid for it. The Ring had not come in at all. Had they smelled a rat?

Sam's cane hovered.

'And ten,' I shouted, waving my hand out of the door.

'Fresh blood,' announced Sam. 'Eight hundred and ten pounds.' He knew it was mine.

There was a long silence. 'Is this to be the price?' he asked.

He kept looking around. More praise was heaped on the dresser. We wanted a clean sale with everything sold. It seemed an age before £820 was bid. We were going to lose money; we needed another thirty pounds to clear ourselves. The bid had come from the bottom of the garden.

'Who is it, John?' I whispered.

Long John eased out of the shed door and leaned on the end of the outhouse.

'Looks like your mate, Elly.'

Prices were high so there would not be a lot in the 'knock-out', but the Ring did like to take any prestige pieces. My heart beat wildly, how far could I take them? Sam was doing his best.

'I shall sell it,' he threatened, 'the nicest piece of furniture ever to come under my hammer.'

Mrs Smythe-Robinson pushed her way through the crowd and stood directly in front of Sam. He was not a tall man and the added inches the box gave him still did not enable him to see over the lady's vast hat. He leaned forward and parted the feathers on the hat with his cane. 'Are you still out there, Mr Ellwood?' he joked. The crowd laughed.

Mrs Smythe-Robinson fixed him with the cold, hard, withering stare she reserves for tradespeople who do not know their place. Sam withered; another pint pot or two and he might have taken her on. He inclined his head to one side and smiled at the formidable woman.

'Do you wish to bid, madam?' he asked politely.

115

Madam wrinkled her nose and waved a gloved hand to disperse Sam's breath. 'Get on with it, man.'

The thought of a rich private buyer taking the best piece in the sale from under their noses put a fresh fire under the Ring's boiler. Elly looked daggers at the woman. The bidding took on a new lease of life, the cane finally coming down in Mrs Smythe-Robinson's favour at £950.

Again Sam smiled, 'Your name, madam?'

She completely ignored him and pushed her way through the crowd towards me. 'How much to deliver it?' she demanded.

I was completely taken aback. 'Five pounds all right?' I asked timidly. The gloved hand thrust a crumpled banknote towards me and off she stomped.

Vicky was clicking away at the calculator. 'Don't forget to add five pounds for the delivery,' I told her as I elaborately straightened the creases out of the note. I rolled it tightly and, gently lifting her long blonde hair, tucked it behind Vicky's left ear. I lay back on the grass and smiled to myself; everything was going well.

The children found us. 'Why can't we have a rabbit? We'll pay for it and look after it.'

'No!' I said again, but this time less definitely. They were quick to perceive the weakness. Plump arms encircled my neck, squeezing it tightly. Two little blonde heads thrust tickling hair into my face.

'Go on, Daddy, go on,' they pleaded.

Finally I relented and they skipped happily alongside me to Long John's van. The cages had been taken out and stacked on the shady side of the vehicle.

'That's the one we want,' they chanted as they dragged me towards the end cage.

It housed the smallest of the rabbits. It climbed the cage front, its little butterfly nose pushing through the wire. It could have sat easily in the palm of my hand. I bent down and lectured them with mock severity.

'How many times do I have to tell you? At an auction sale you never show interest in anything you really want.' Their little upturned faces saddened, so I gave them a broad wink. 'We'll see what we can do.'

We had had a good day and I resolved to buy that rabbit if it cost a tenner.

The ferrets had been set apart from the rabbits, which were their natural prey. Sleek effective killers, they were excited. They poured themselves over each other as they boiled around in the cage, continually sniffing the air. Sam's box was brought and set in front of the cages. He didn't mount it. After another 'pot of tea' such giddy heights were uninviting.

'We are now shelling the liveshtock for a neighbour.' He belched politely into the back of his hand and beamed at the crowd.

Long John unhooked the wire from the front of the end box and fished out the little rabbit. He held out its kicking body at arm's length. 'A good 'un, a pure-bred English doe; make a big rabbit, this.'

The little struggling body fell from his hands. It dropped to the ground quite unhurt and started to nibble the grass.

'Shtand back, shtand back,' shouted Sam, weaving gracefully from side to side. 'We don't want anybody lamed. Tha 'ad better put a halter on it, John, before it does some damage.' The crowd laughed and Sam warmed to his task.

'Eddie! Come over here and give John a hand with this 'ere animile,' he called to his clerk. The tiny rabbit crouched between Long John's enormous boots. 'It's not a kicker, is it, John?' he enquired.

Long John grinned.

'Now we're shelling this 'ere animile with all faults – don't come running back to me if it bites yer legs off.'

I offered a pound for the rabbit. Sam grinned broadly as he brought down the cane.

'A brave man, a brave man.'

The children scooped it up and bore it happily off to the van. After another 'pot of tea' Sam was quite drunk. He staggered to Long John's van and lay full length in the back, oblivious of the accumulated dung from rabbits, ferrets and the odd goat. Long John finished the auction himself. He held out each animal in turn and waited until he heard an acceptable bid. His long arms would fling out towards the bidder.

'Yours.'

I bought another rabbit for a pound and carried it off to the van.

The children were delighted. I watched them feeding choice pieces of succulent grass into the little chewing mouths. Vicky came up behind me and prodded me in the back with her pen.

'And who is supposed to be watching the grandfather clock?' she asked in a chastening tone. My God, I had completely forgotten about the clock. 'It's all right,' she said, seeing the look of concern on my face. 'The glorious Mr Ellwood paid £600 for it.'

Relief swept over me. It was a handsome price for a little thirty-hour clock and we were well into profit. The crowd began to disperse, as Long John helped me to lift Mrs Smythe-Robinson's dresser into the van. I wrapped it carefully in blankets; I had no wish to incur the wrath of that formidable woman.

The agreement with Sam was that we would settle up on the day. The cashier, a thin, humourless, meticulous man, would not be hurried. I shared the last of the doorstop sandwiches with Long John, then we carried the inert Sam and laid him out in the back of his Land-Rover. The cashier appeared with the balance sheet and two cheques, one for me and one for Long John. If I was delighted with mine, Long John was more than pleased with his. He had constant money problems. The clerk had deducted Sam's fee and fifteen pounds for 'peripheral expenses' – whatever they were. I wasn't going to argue, it had been a really good day.

Long John did a mock rumba across the garden towards us, a rabbit in one hand and a bottle in the other. A fat cheque and a little 'nectar of the gods' really brought a man out. He thrust the rabbit towards the laughing children.

'Here, I can't take the little bugger back to live on its own, can I?' The bottle of Swaledale Lightning dropped in my lap. 'A leetle celebration,' he laughed and thrust his hands deep into the smock pockets. 'We've had a good day, owd lad.'

Tommy Watts stood in the centre of the garden, leaning heavily on two sticks. He looked around him in bewilderment. Fatty Batty's men were loading his van with the clock and the Windsor chairs. A man and two women hoisted the heavy kist on to a flimsy roofrack and festooned it with ropes. A young couple happily juggled the set of dining chairs into a small hatchback. A black-haired woman with two small children carefully packed the Staffordshire figures into a washing basket. All was activity.

One far-off summer between the wars, Tommy had paid court to Aunt Flo. He was one of the few people she would speak to after she had gone funny. His puzzled face looked up at Long John.

'I never knew she had all this stuff. Where did she keep it?'

Long John's beard was split with a wide grin as he bent down to the old man's ear. 'We found it all in that little cupboard under the stairs,' he explained.

Chapter 12

Rabbit was the son of Teal, and Teal was the son of the legendary Widgeon. Every poacher had his *nom de guerre*; it afforded him a certain protection when tongues were loosened in the ale house and it was his shibboleth. Widgeon had been the king of the local poachers. Sometimes on a bitter winter's night, when rain beat a tattoo on the taproom window and the fire burned brightly, men would draw their chairs and stools around it and the talk would turn to poaching. It would not be long before the name of Widgeon was on the old men's lips. Only the old men remembered him, for he was old when they were boys, but the stories they told of him gave them caste because they had known him.

Widgeon had poached the surrounding countryside for three score years. He had the secrets of calling hares to within a dozen paces of himself and of how the sleek brown trout could be brought to the net, a dozen at a time. He knew the ways of the fox and the badger and where the geese fed when the moon was full and the wind was from the west. He knew how to take a duck from the flighting pond without ruffling the still water and how to keep the red-legged grouse from rising above the line net. He knew where to find the freshwater crayfish and where he could fill his cap with corncrake's eggs. He could neither read nor write, but what use has a man for pens and paper when he has knowledge such as this?

In his long years poaching, Widgeon had only been taken once. His companion that cold, moonless night had stumbled into a trip-wire, setting off an alarm gun. The keepers had surrounded the wood but Widgeon had given them the slip. His companion had been caught and the burly second keeper had made free with his cudgel about the poor fellow's body. Widgeon, on hearing his cries, had returned to assist him but had soon been overpowered and borne off in triumph to the police station. He did his thirty days in York. Thirty days without the wind on his face or the spring of the heather under his foot, and he had resolved that no matter what, he would never be taken again.

In the last year of Queen Victoria's reign there had been a terrible accident at the quarry. The powderman had laid his charges well and the rumble of explosions had peeled an avalanche of rock from the quarry face. When the dust had settled and the men had gone to clear the rock a tall column, left unsupported by a natural fissure, had collapsed, killing two men.

Both men were from the village and both left a widow with a young family to bring up single-handed. In those days the authorities were not so free with their monies and many a morning the women awoke, the instant worry of feeding their family that day pushing all else from their minds. But Widgeon had passed in the night, and freshly killed rabbit and a sizeable turnip lay on each doorstep.

The squire at that time had been the second Fairbrother to own the Estate. A brusque, heavy-drinking man, he was disliked by all. One day, Widgeon had found him unconscious by the river. The worse for drink, he had put his cob at the high hedge but the animal had refused, ditching his rider and making off. Widgeon had carried the squire back to the Hall, leaving him propped against the heavy panelled door. His gold-topped riding crop was tucked into the top of his boot but the guineas had gone from his pocket. Widgeon had many allies: the carter and the shepherd would keep a watchful eye on the constable for him, and more than one farmer's wife would deliver his pheasants to Lalbeck hidden in the bottom of her butter basket.

As the new century progressed, poaching became more difficult. The big Edwardian shooting parties with their drives and battues demanded more game for the guns. Keepering became more intensive and the penalties when caught were more severe. By the time Widgeon saw his son off to the Kaiser's war it was almost impossible to make a living by poaching. Teal returned with an oak leaf pinned to his medal ribbons and married Elsie Watts. Exactly a year after he had brushed the mud of Flanders from his boots, Elsie presented him with a son, Joseph. Teal, with a wife and child to support, took a job at the quarry.

Once the child was old enough to leave with Widgeon, the jolly Elsie went to work in the kitchen at the Hall. The old man had been a widower for many years and the boy filled a void in his life; they became inseparable. They had the same pace, for although Widgeon was now bent and slow and the boy quick, with limbs as light as thistledown, the latter, with his insatiable curiosity, flitted constantly about the old man. As the doe sedately walks along the forest track her fawn prances into the undergrowth on each side of her, nibbling grasses, reaching up to sample the tender bough and stopping to test the air with tiny coal-black nostrils. They both enter the clearing together. So it was with the old man and the boy.

Widgeon planned the days carefully. He knew he did not have long and there was so much to teach the boy. He would sit at the top of the lane, bread and cheese in his pockets and the dogs at his feet, waiting for the boy to come out of school. They would set off on to the moor, the boy chattering away and the old man listening and smiling as he stabbed his stick into the steep track. Widgeon wanted the boy to know every inch of his territory. When his legs ached he would sit heavily on the ling and, with a wave of his stick, point out some feature on the sky-line.

'Over there, there's a little beck that runs down that ghyll. There's a pool about there.' The stick would stab with short jerky movements and the boy would stand silently staring at where it pointed.

'In them trees a pair of herons nest.' Widgeon would sink back, resting on one elbow, slowly feeding bits of cheese and bread into his toothless mouth as the boy ran off, the dogs at his heels. He would return breathless and, dropping to the ground beside the old man, describe all that he had seen. The old man would nod and smile.

It was on one of these summer evenings that the dogs had put up a rabbit. A full-grown buck, it had leaped and twisted over the clumps of heather, gaining from the little terriers. In its panic it ignored the boy and, turning back from the scree, had run to within a stick's length of him. Young Joseph clubbed it to death and ran proudly to the old man, holding aloft the bloodstained body.

'Rabbit! Rabbit!' he shouted excitedly.

Widgeon had paunched the rabbit and, keeping the liver and kidneys attached to the carcass, he had thrown a handful of warm entrails to the eager dogs. All the way home the boy repeatedly thwacked his stick into clumps of heather and gorse, showing the old man how he had killed his rabbit.

Elsie rolled out pastry on the pine tabletop as Teal fed sticks under the oven. The boy was allowed to stay up late that night. He sat at the table bright-eyed, his little clenched fists tightly holding his knife and fork to attention as Elsie folded her pinny and brought the hot pie from the oven. As it was his first kill and he had put the meat on the table, Teal served him first.

'Rabbit pie for Rabbit Joe,' said old Widgeon, and Rabbit Joe it has been ever since.

'Rabbit's yer man,' pronounced Charlie in The Ship when I had finished my tale of woe about the moles. Try as we could, the traps we set were never sprung and the progression of molehills across the field was beginning to give it the appearance of being ploughed.

Wearing old gardening gloves, we carefully cut into the main runs and set our traps. Smoothing out the bottom of the run with a dessert spoon and tearing the sod with our hands, we packed it gently around the trap to stop the light getting in. Moles are nearly blind but their sense of smell is acute. The traps, the old carving knife we used and the spoon with the cunningly bent handle we left in the garden to weather along with the gloves. A man who handles cows or sheep cannot catch the 'mouldy'; the scent of him, no matter how he tries to disguise it, sets the mole on its guard. Only in early spring, when the moles are mating or 'chasing', might he have some luck if a

125

female is bolted into a trap by a pursuing male. Some advised us to poison the moles and others to gas them. Neither way appealed to us, so I took Charlie's advice and went to see Rabbit.

Rabbit's cottage was surprisingly neat for a man who had lived on his own for many years. His wife had left him after a couple of years of marriage, taking their daughter with her. Rabbit was a well-set-up fellow and the wedding photograph on the sideboard showed him as a slim young man with raven-black hair. The plump girl alongside him, self-consciously hanging on to his arm, was obviously well pregnant, the meagre bouquet failing to conceal the round full belly. She was a Brockway from Sottenghyll – a surly family. Old Ambrose and his three sons had not been pleased when Phyllis, no longer able to hide her roundness, had tearfully disclosed the father of her child to be. Amby had sent for Rabbit, and when Amby sent for you, you went. Rabbit had felt eyes upon him as soon as he had left the moor road and started up the narrow track alongside the ghyll. The three sons were lounging around the farmyard and returned his nervous greeting with silent scowls.

Old Amby was sat at the kitchen table, his coat over the chair back. Rabbit had nodded at him, but the old man had just stared silently back and fished into his waistcoat pocket. He had produced three half-crowns and set them carefully at one side of the table, and at the opposite side he had set a ten-bore cartridge loaded with number four shot. Rabbit had looked at it and winced. God! How that would tear the flesh off a man's bones.

Amby had stared at Rabbit. 'Well, which is it to be?'

Rabbit knew full well the intent; three half-crowns was the price of a marriage licence.

They were married a month later and the child was born a month after that. If it had been a boy things might have been different, but Rabbit had not been too put out when he had come in from a night's poaching to find them both gone. Phyllis could neither read nor write, so there had been no farewell note. Instead she had told a neighbour, 'Tell the selfish sod I never want to see him again and if he comes after us our lads'll have him.'

Rabbit had settled down once more with his dogs and ferrets to lead the life of a country bachelor. He was of the firm belief that a man could work too hard and that the secret of true happiness lay in getting the mix of poaching and drinking just right. He did the rabbiting and molecatching for the Estate, who believed he was less of a nuisance on its payroll than off. They were right, for Rabbit never poached the Estate land; the annual retainer he received and the money he earned beating were too precious to jeopardize.

Rabbit settled himself into the Windsor chair. 'Trouble wi mouldies, eh? Aye, I'll have a look at 'em.'

'How much do you want for clearing them, Rabbit?'

The weather-beaten face cracked into a smile. 'Depends how many I ketch.' He waved me towards an armchair. Its seat covering had long gone and a small sack stuffed with dog hair covered the springs. 'I'll show thi summet now.' He opened an oak salt box and took out a tobacco pouch. It was covered in a fine white fur. 'Does tha know what that is?' Before I could make any comment he went on. 'That's made out of albino mouldies – that's white 'uns – old Widgeon got 'em, must be fifty year ago, down on that land you have from Nellie May.'

He put the pouch in my hands and stood with his back to the fire. The tiny room was warm and smelled of dogs and cooking. The stone floor was covered with hooky rugs and the walls were cluttered with yellowed sporting prints. Stuffed owls and other birds of prey stared, glass-eyed, from their square cases. From the beams hung fishing rods and gaffs and set on the wall above the powder cupboard was a mantrap. The huge deadly teeth were wired back to the wall. Rabbit saw me looking at it.

'Nearly got Widgeon one night, so he brought it home.'

I admired the pouch, with its incredibly soft fur covering, and handed it back. 'It's nice, very nice.'

Rabbit took the pouch and turned it over in his huge hands. 'Tell thi what I'll do. I'll clear thi mouldies and if I gits one of them, I'll do it for nowt; if not, it's a fiver.'

I thought the chances of Rabbit getting an albino mole were remote to say the least, and a fiver did not seem too dear for the work involved, so I agreed.

After a couple of days, sleek little fat bodies began to be nailed to the barn door.

We raked out the molehills and within a fortnight no more appeared. There were nine moles nailed on the door. They were beginning to decompose and the stench from them was terrible. I gave it another week and, when no more little bodies or molehills were forthcoming, went off to see Rabbit.

'You got nine, I see. I think I owe you a fiver.'

Rabbit grinned. 'Tha owes me nowt.' He reached a board down from the mantelpiece. On it were tacked two white moleskins.

Chapter 13

If we were expecting Canary Mary and it was a fine warm morning, I would take my coffee and sit on the flat-topped wall at the side of the shop. I would keep my eyes trained on the gap between the Colonel's house and the Martins's tall poplars until I saw the little egg-yellow Citroën 2CV busying itself along the lane to Ramsthwaite. I would then take my mug into the kitchen, warn Vicky she was on her way and station myself at the bottom of the village green ready to receive her. Mary's eyesight was not as good as it should have been, and she flatly refused to negotiate the wash-fold and drive the car up to the shop.

Canary Mary, like royalty, always announced her visits well beforehand, and three days earlier a scented primrose notelet had dropped through our letterbox. She had refused to use the telephone ever since her little dispute with the GPO, when she had painted the telephone box outside her cottage that delightful shade of lemon. The boorish little man they had sent along had steadfastly refused to acknowledge that it now blended harmoniously with her sand-coloured picket fence and her cadmium-yellow door.

'Telephone boxes is red,' he'd kept saying.

When the box had been returned to its garish colour, she had consoled herself by growing a winter-flowering jasmine against it and having her telephone taken out. She would not deal with people who had no colour sense.

Mary was a creature of habit. If she wasn't doing a flea-market she rose at ten, fed her two ginger toms, filled the little porcelain troughs in the aviary, breakfasted on an egg and an orange and then, still in her citrine nightdress, she arranged herself on the gold dralon *chaise longue* and read the day's news-papers. Lunch was always at somebody else's house. That day we were the favoured ones.

I opened the door of the Citroën with a flourish and handed her out. She was wearing a bright yellow trench coat with matching floppy hat, over a cream polo-neck sweater and beige skirt. Her shoes, sensible brogues with just the hint of a heel, were bright yellow. It was impossible to get the right colour, she had told Vicky, so she bought any that suited her extra-broad feet and painted them. A double rivulet of amber beads appeared from under her hazel hair to join together in a knot of soft winking light, before cascading down the chasm formed between her full round breasts.

'You look lovely, Mary.'

She lifted up her dark brown eyes to mine and her sensuous mouth, its outline extended and sharpened by generous appli-cations of lipstick, split into a wide grin. 'Thank you, pet. Be a duck and bring the box.'

I reached into the car. It was warm and heady with scent; not a cheap scent, for there was nothing cheap about Mary.

She was the Queen of the Fleamarkets. The box was heavy and, as I struggled up the green behind her ample body, she raised a plump arm to give a bangle-jangling wave to everyone she saw.

She was so warm and outgoing, such a caring, loving, sunny woman. Children and animals adored her, men loved her and, with the exception of Little Petal, women liked her. We have never discovered what soured the relationship between the two big girls, but I have a suspicion it stemmed from the time Little Petal emptied the contents of the biscuit barrel on to the kitchen table and took all the custard creams. There is no deep enmity between them; each just refuses to acknowledge the existence of the other. Petal in her dark-brown rumpled caftans and Mary in her crisp yellow outfits were soon dubbed 'Prunes and Custard' by the villagers.

Mary settled herself into the broad-arm Windsor and, with the cat on her lap, kept up a constant chatter as I unpacked the box. Vicky glanced anxiously at the clock and clattered plates on to the table. The children would soon be home for lunch and we had to get the spicy bits of gossip before they burst in and commandeered their beloved Auntie Mary. She had brought a good bronze Japanese *koro* and a three-piece silver tea service – not heavy and a bit late, but a nice elegant set. I put them back in the box and placed it carefully on the dresser.

'Nice stuff, Mary.' She interrupted her chatter with a little nod and a smile. We would discuss prices later.

We were having lemon sole with potato croquettes and garden peas. A big, sticky, sugar-frosted apple pie sat warming on the oven top and the Wensleydale waited, creamy and silent, under the blue-and-white cheese cover.

The children had seen the yellow car at the bottom of the green and ran pell-mell in a wide arc round the corner of the farmhouse to jostle together in the doorway, before hurling themselves across the kitchen and on to Mary's lap. The cat slipped to the floor and flicked an angry tail. Two ample yellow arms enfolded the happy pair.

'My chicks, my little cuddly chicks.' The plump arms swayed the children from side to side. Peter, after revelling in the soft scented warmth for as long as he dared, shuffled from her knee and stood with his arm around the back of the chair. Sally, no burgeoning masculinity to inhibit her, curled herself tighter against Mary, her little innocent hand sought out the beads and swung them gently so they caught the light from the fire.

'We're doing the Romans,' Peter ventured.

'Silly people,' Mary replied. 'Fancy choosing purple for the imperial colour.'

Lunch was noisy. The cat had climbed back on to Mary's lap and was fed little morsels of fish as she told the children a delicious little story about Miss Wells's first boyfriend, for she had been at school with Annie Wells.

The women and children had a warm giggling intimacy which, while not excluding me, didn't embrace me completely, so I acted as waiter. I cut the apple pie and, placing a slice of cheese on each piece, handed it round.

Mary laughed. 'Apple pie without cheese. It's like a kiss without a squeeze.' She pulled Peter to her and gave him a noisy kiss. Peter gave his shy little smile and the faintest hint of a blush crossed his cheeks.

The school bell was ringing as we waved the children off across the village green. 'Mind the road,' shouted Mary, and they joined hands to cross before turning to give her a last wave and disappear through the wrought-iron gates.

We settled in front of the fire with our coffee and, when Mary had screwed a long cigarette into her amber holder and sent the first grey wisps of smoke drifting up to the creel, I asked her what she wanted for the tea set and *koro*.

'The silver is Sheffield 1903, and that vase thing,' she paused and wrinkled her brow, 'what exactly is it? I haven't seen one before.'

'It's a vessel used on Shinto shrines to contain token offerings to the gods.' She pursed her mouth then sent more smoke to percolate through the creel. I got the impression she did not rate it very highly. It was a good mid-nineteenth-century bronze one, standing on three tall feet and with finely cast decoration. The cover supported well-modelled figures of a man and a monkey.

Vicky washed up and went to dust around the shop, leaving Mary and me to do the wrangling. It was two hours and several cups of coffee before we agreed on a price. I thought she over-rated the tea service and underrated the *koro*. I paid her in cash and entered the items in the stockbook.

The sun had some real warmth in it as we walked her down the green to her car.

'Be a duck and put the roof down for me.' I rolled back the canvas hood and the car rocked as she lowered her weight into it. A lipstick appeared and the redefined mouth smiled up at me. 'I have a beautiful conversation settee that might interest you. I've nothing on this week. Pop down and have a look at it.'

We waved until she was out of sight. Ted had been watching us from the byre door and while Vicky hurried on back to the shop I stopped to have a word with him. He nodded in the direction the little car had taken.

'By gum, lad, but 'ar could fettle yon.'

Mary could be a naughty girl. Once when she had fancied an early nineteenth-century kutani spill vase with orange ground at an auction, she had stuck a 'made in Taiwan' label on the bottom during the viewing and it had been knocked down to her for a fraction of its real value.

More than once she had promised us a piece of furniture, only to sell it to some passing dealer before we could get down to see her; so the very next day we had the van waiting at the school gates for the children.

Mary opened the door for us sporting a magnificent black eye. She raised her hands to fend off our questions and ushered us into the sitting room.

'Had a little bang in my car, but I'm all right.' The two cats, Amber and Topaz, were curled asleep on the *chaise longue* so Vicky dropped into the big chintz-covered armchair while I squatted on the brown leather pouffe. The children settled themselves in front of the fire on the thick saffron hearthrug. Mary excused herself and waddled off to the kitchen.

The sitting room, with its warm yellow fabrics, its ochre walls and stripped pine furniture beeswaxed to a delicate honey, was like boxed sunshine. Although it was not a cold day, a bright fire burned in the grate and through the half-open French windows came the chatter of Mary's canaries. The oven door clunked in the kitchen and a warm aroma of fresh baking drifted into the room. The children looked at each other, and turned to grin at us.

'Fat rascals,' they chorused.

Mary heard them and laughed. 'You're right, my little chickens, what wicked little noses you must have.'

Vicky pulled herself out of the chair and went to help in the kitchen, impelled by that need that all women seem to have to be part of the domestic scene.

The black-eyed half of Mary's face appeared round the door. 'The settee is down in the wash-house, duck. Have a peek at it.'

The tiny walled back garden was half taken up with the aviary and a big Rex rabbit shook its dewlap as it grazed the strip of lawn which ran down to the wash-house. Inside, shelves were stacked with Mary's fleamarket stock and in a corner, beside the settee, stood a Chippendale-style silver table in pale yellow undercoat. On the window sill tins of paint, representing every hue of the beloved colour, stood ranked three deep.

The settee was a mediocre one. It had recently been reupholstered in kingfisher blue and its rail back and legs were ebonized – not a good seller. I watched the canaries until Vicky called me back into the sitting room.

Plates of 'fat rascals' sat on the chair arms as Mary bent over the table pouring tea from a Clarice Cliff teapot. The trick with 'fat rascals' is to bring them to the table when they have just enough residual heat in them to melt the butter such that it drops into the little ridges and crevices. Too cold and the butter stays in its slicked wedges and curls; too warm and it flows, a sticky gee, on to the fingers.

Mary's were just right. She scooped up a cat and dropped on to the *chaise longue*. It was time for the tale of the car and the black eye. 'Well, after I had been to your place yesterday I went up to Long John's and had a few drinkies.' I shuddered. The combination of Mary's poor eyesight and Swaledale Lightning didn't bode well for the little yellow car. Topaz licked a buttery forefinger. 'Well, I got down the track all right but opposite the Post Office there was this horrid little wall.'

'Was?'

She didn't answer. She wiped a little finger along the butter and offered it to Amber who, realizing he was missing something, had uncurled himself, stretched, and now stood with his two front paws on Mary's thigh. She began to cry big fat tears. 'Oh! Oh! My little car, it's all bashed in at one side and Mr Dinsdale says it's going to cost an awful lot of money.'

The children climbed on to the *chaise*, one at each side of her and, curtly dismissing the cats, put their arms around her. 'Don't worry, Auntie. Mr Dinsdale will make it better.'

Mary brightened and turned her warm smile on me. 'Well, what do you think of the settee? Lovely, isn't it?'

I didn't think it was lovely but I didn't tell her so, I just asked her the price. She whispered a figure which was twenty-five pounds over the top. I shook my head. The tears welled up again and the children glared at me as they consoled the sobbing woman. It looked as though I was going to have to contribute to the 'awful lot of money'. I counted out the notes on to the pine dresser.

It was almost dark when we arrived home, the hens had gone to roost and Elspeth peeped a bright inquisitive head through the orchard fence. As Vicky got the children ready for bed I went into the shop, got the stockbook out and raised the price of the tea service fifteen pounds and the *koro* by ten pounds. Somebody has to pay for the world's beautiful people.

Chapter 14

It was late October and already the leaves had fallen to fill the gutters and stick in the brown dried grass. There had been a light frost, and a pale morning sunshine filtered through the mist as I took the milk can off its hook and made for the orchard.

Elspeth was waiting at the gate, her coat wet with dew and plumes of vapour blowing from her pink nostrils. She trotted alongside me across the yard to the lean-to near the apple house, which we'd fitted out as a goat house. I had built a small wooden milking platform and set a manger at one end, and she leaped readily on to the platform with a clatter of hooves. I put a scoop of dairy nuts into the manger and she set to work on them eagerly while I washed her udder.

She was in her first lactation and was milking well for a young goat. Browsers by nature, goats need a good deal of nutriment to give of their best and we never stinted the dairy nuts and hay; in fact at one point we had to watch that she didn't get over-fat. She gave five pints a day; the biggest milking was the early morning one, when I could coax nearly three pints from her swollen udder.

I put the stainless-steel milk can under her and set to work. Even on cold mornings her udder was warm. This morning it seemed a little flaccid and not as well rounded as usual, and I had no more than a pint or so of frothy milk in the can before she was dry. I stripped each teat with finger and thumb and stood back to look at her. She was bright and healthy, her eyes were clear and she had cleaned her manger. I ran my hands over her, looked at her mouth and nostrils, legs and feet. There was nothing at all wrong with her, she was a perfectly healthy goat. I was baffled by the sudden drop in the milk yield.

I turned her back into the orchard and leaned on the gate, watching her awhile. She wandered around the orchard nibbling here and there, perfectly happy. The country folk had it that hedgehogs drew milk from goats in the night, but I didn't believe this. It wasn't a blocked teat, as she had given equally from both. I resolved to seek out Ted that night and ask his opinion. I set the milk can on the draining board as Vicky swung the griddle from the fire and forked the bacon and eggs on to plates.

'Look in there,' I said. 'I don't know what's happened to her.' Normally we had more than enough milk for ourselves and the surplus went to the animals. As we ate our breakfast, I went over and over in my mind what could have happened.

'You don't believe that hedgehog thing, do you?' said Vicky.

I shook my head. I couldn't see it being possible. Hedgehogs will readily take milk from a dish, but they are voracious eaters and their long snouts would make any sucking action difficult, even if Elspeth could be induced to lie still.

138

The children came in from feeding the rabbits and Vicky bundled them into their coats ready for school. As the door closed behind them, I drew my chair up to the fire and lit a pipe. I couldn't get the problem of Elspeth's lack of milk out of my mind. If there had been a gradual tapering off of yield I would have looked for a problem in diet or parasites of some kind, but this sudden drop had me completely mystified. I finished my pipe and rapped it out on the iron reckon. Vicky was late back from taking the children to school. Even on the most inclement of mornings the mothers would have a few minutes' gossip round the school gates before starting for home, but it was now twenty past nine and she still hadn't appeared. I started the van and drove it round to the front of the shop; we had a delivery to do that morning.

'Have you seen our new neighbours?' Vicky asked, pointing to Nellie May's as she arrived back at the shop.

Over the high stone wall I would just see the green canvas tilt of a bow-top caravan. It would be Nellie May's nephew. Thomas Lascelles Bendelow, commonly known as Apple Tom, always called in to see his aunt after his annual pilgrimage to Appleby Fair. We'd heard mixed reports of him from the villagers; some liked the easy-going rogue, some detested him. It seemed to depend on whether or not you were a gardener and poultry keeper, for on his annual visits a few vegetables would disappear from each back garden and a hen or two would be unaccounted for.

I jumped into the cab and was about to turn the key in the ignition, but I couldn't contain my curiosity any longer. The delivery could wait a few more minutes. I skirted the barn and climbed the little hill behind the apple house. Leaning on the wall, I had full view of Nellie May's.

Pulled under the lee of the wall was a Yorkshire bow-top caravan. A plume of smoke rose from the cast-iron chimney and on the steps between the dropped shafts sat a small, grubby child. He clutched a tin mug of milk in his hands and there was a white rime about his thin mouth. As his dark-brown eyes surveyed me silently, it suddenly became apparent to me where the rest of Elspeth's bounty had gone.

The vardo was immaculate. Although the green canvas tilt was faded and stained, the panelled sides were a rich emerald, lined and decorated in yellow and red. Past the thin shoulders of the child I could see the shining black of the cast-iron stove and the rich mahogany of the interior fittings. It was the type of vardo which had been made in the Leeds area until the 1930s and was favoured by the northern travelling folk more than the heavier and less stable Reading type. A flat cart stood with its shafts in the air and two skewbald horses were tethered at the bottom of the common, where a thin woman spread bright clean washing on the gorse bushes to dry.

Apple Tom was nowhere to be seen. I had heard many tales of this character and was keen to see him. I lay against the loose stone wall, the autumn sunshine at my back, for a quarter of an hour or more. The thin woman finished hanging out her washing and disappeared inside the vardo. The small child was still sitting on the steps, and fixed me with an uncomfortable stare. I could hear the small French ormolu clock in the shop chime ten with its little tinny bell. I had to make my delivery, so I set off up the dale at a fair speed.

Vicky had lunch ready when I pulled into the yard. We had had duck the night before and she had put the remaining meat into sandwiches with a salad. We took our coffee and sat in the orchard. Elspeth came up and nuzzled us with her warm soft nose, and the hens formed a circle round us looking for titbits.

With the dry summer the peas had not filled out properly, but the apples were full and ripe and as they fell to the ground Elspeth devoured them readily. All the trees were old and past their prime. As we sat in the orchard discussing replanting it, we heard the shop bell ring. Vicky had had a busy morning: she had been making jam and bottling beetroot and the bell had been ringing constantly. I set my mug of coffee on the wall, out of the reach of Elspeth, and made my way down to the shop.

A tall, gaunt fellow, nut-brown and wearing a battered trilby, stood there with the small child I had seen on the steps of the caravan. It was obviously Apple Tom.

'Now then, mister,' he said, 'you've got some nice stuff in here.'

I was instantly wary. I knew he had a terrible reputation and as I ran my eyes around the shop I wondered what he could have pocketed in the half minute or so it had taken me to get in from the orchard. He went round the shop slowly, looking at everything.

'You must get all sorts of stuff,' he said. I told him we did. 'Would you be having any clothes now, sir?'

We had just done a part house clearance at Richmond. It was the remains of the estate of a deceased judge and there had been two wardrobes full of sober but high-quality clothes. Apple Tom picked through these. He came out with a fine three-piece worsted suit.

'How much for this, mister?'

'Three pounds,' I replied quickly.

'It's very reasonable, mister,' he said, placing it on a chair in the corner.

He picked out two shirts and a pair of brogue shoes. 'A pound,' I shouted, before he could say anything. He grinned and placed them on the pile. A good but dated trench coat followed, at two pounds. Apple Tom bundled up the clothes and his son stood proudly with the shoes.

'Call it a fiver for the lot, mister,' he said with a cheeky grin. I held out my hand and he pressed a crumpled note into it.

I climbed back up to the orchard to my cold coffee and told Vicky of my dealings with Apple Tom. We were quite pleased because we could never find outlets for clothing and they usually ended up as free gifts to local charity shops.

I spent that afternoon at a farm sale at Hysop Grange. The children were back from school and tucking into egg and chips when I arrived home. Vicky cut two thick slices of ham and dropped them into the griddle pan. It was barely five o'clock, the sky was overcast and a heavy cloud over the fell brought the first chill of winter. The kitchen was warm and cosy with the smell of cooking. Drawing my broad-arm Windsor up to the fire, I watched the ham sizzle and brown in the griddle.

Sally pushed her plate away, her food half-eaten; she was a picky eater. She gathered the cat in her arms and squatted on the tab rug beside me. 'We've been to see the gypsies today,' she said.

I lighted my pipe from a glowing taper, remembering I must lock up the goat. 'What did you think of them?' I said.

'They're nice people,' she replied, 'but they use some funny words.'

Vicky turned the ham on the griddle, it sizzled and sparks of fat flew up the chimney. I dined with the plate on my knee, just a slice of ham and some homemade bread. The sky had cleared; it was a pale moonlit sky. I took the dogs out and locked up the poultry. I went to the orchard and caught Elspeth by her collar. She pulled and tugged as I walked her across the yard to the goat house. We had no lock on the door, so I shot the bolt home and tied it with baler twine. We'd see how she milked in the morning.

As we sat around the fire that night the talk again turned to gypsies. Apparently, the boy I'd seen sat on the vardo steps was called Roddy. He'd filled the children's ears with tales of his many exploits, and these the children babbled forth to us. Vicky and I were a little apprehensive, wondering if any of the bad language had been picked up, but the travellers were wise in these ways – they had realized we were a soft touch and wouldn't want to jeopardize it in any way. We heard of Roddy's expertise at trapping and living off the country. He'd promised to teach Peter how to tickle trout and had ridden the little skew-ball gelding bareback over the common at full tilt to demonstrate his prowess as a horseman, but the one thing that had really impressed the children was the fact that he had only been to school for three weeks in the whole of his life. 'School learning,' he had declared with great dignity, 'is a waste of time.' Vicky hurriedly countered this by pointing out that they had a hard life and missed a lot of the things that a stable home and steady income brought.

As we tucked them into bed in the caravan that night, the talk was still of gypsies. The children were adamant that they had a better life than ours and both were firmly resolved to become gypsies when they grew up. As I turned down the light I told them that real gypsies had to eat hedgehogs, slept with only one blanket over them on the coldest of winter nights and never had birthdays. I could see a little doubt cross their faces about their proposed future.

Vicky and I had our supper in the kitchen. We wondered how long the gypsies would stay. Although I had made the goat and hens secure, I had simply herded the ducks into a corner of the Dutch barn and made a makeshift pen of corrugated sheets and bales of straw. Apple Tom was a notorious poultry thief. He always raided the coops late on the last night of his stay and was off at the crack of dawn the morning after. I wondered if he cooked ducks in the old gypsy way of encasing them in clay, feathers and all, and baking them in the embers of the fire. We had a motley flock of ducks: several Khaki Campbells, several pairs of Silver Appleyards and quite a number of Muscovys. The Muscovys were hardy ducks and had bred well. They were mainly ornamental, but made very good eating. We went to bed that night knowing we were at the mercy of Apple Tom.

The following morning I rose earlier than usual. The ducks were intact in their pen and the hens all accounted for. The binder twine on the goat house had not been tampered with and Elspeth verified this as she leapt on to the milking platform, for her udder was full and round. I gave her an extra handful of dairy nuts to compensate for a night of confinement and the milk frothed into the little pail to its normal level. I turned her into the orchard and she gambolled around, shaking her head as if she had been away from her favourite haunt for days.

'Milking all right, is she?'

I turned round to see Apple Tom leaning over the wall. 'She seems to milk a bit better when she's kept up at night,' I said with a wry smile.

He gave me a broad grin in return. 'Is that your gallower in Aunt Nellie's field?' he asked.

Topic was a registered Dales mare and I was not too happy

to have her described as a gallower. He pulled a small tin from his top pocket and rolled a cigarette, lighting it with a gas lighter. He seemed to want to talk so I put the can of milk on the caravan steps and strolled across to the wall. The two skew-balls were tethered to the gorse bushes and nosed about among the sparse ling.

'They seem a sturdy pair,' I said, nodding towards them.

'Aye, they're all right, but you want to watch that one of yours, she's a bit overweight. Does it do much work?'

'No, we just have a little coup cart for her, she shifts a few logs and a bit of muck; she's mainly for the children.'

'You want to watch her in spring if she's not working much. It's over-good grass down there and she could get a touch of laminitis. You want to bring her up here for a touch of hard living.' He nodded towards the common.

I had heard of Apple Tom's deep knowledge of horse ailments and their cures and I was tempted to draw him forth a bit. 'What if she does get a touch of laminitis?' I asked.

Apple Tom turned his back to the wall and stared across the common. A few moments of silence followed as he drew deeply on his hand-rolled cigarette. I wondered if I had breached some form of etiquette, asking the master for some of his secrets. At length he broke the silence. 'Malt vinegar; not this acidy vinegar you get today, but real malt vinegar. You warms it up so you can just stand your hand in it, then you rubs her chest and shoulders and legs right well under the armpits – rub it right well in and put a lot on – rug her up and run her round until she sweats; give her nowt to eat, just let her stand rugged up and she'll be as right as rain in the morning.'

Another long silence followed as he puffed away at his cigarette. Nellie May came out of her cottage and wandered up to the caravan. She gave a cursory nod in our direction before she went inside. The small gelding lifted its head and whinnied towards the top of the common to where young Roddy appeared, a couple of rabbits slung over his shoulder. Without looking at his father, he flung them on to the grass before us. Apple Tom looked at them approvingly.

'I'll see to them. You yoke up the gelding,' said Apple Tom. Roddy did his bidding without a word in reply. 'That gelding was coughing bad when I bought him, but I soon had him cured. All he wanted was liquorice powder and a good hot mash. I kept him off hay for a while.'

The sun had broken through the low haze. He lifted his foot and settled it comfortably against the wall; his cigarette had long since gone out but he still sucked at it noisily. He went through every horse ailment in the book. He told me how to cure thrush, croup, glanders, constipation, how to stop a 'runner' with a rope bridle wrapped with hedgehog skin and how to cure a 'stopper' by weaving straw into its tail. He told me how to cure a capped hock and how to draw an abscess with a poultice of fresh cow dung.

Young Roddy had put the gelding to the flat cart and led it up towards us. It stood ready for work, chomping at its bit. I noticed there was a large swelling on its offside jaw and asked Apple Tom what it was. He sucked again on the dead cigarette.

'Ah now,' he said, 'I don't know what that is. The vet's coming to look at that tonight.'

We saw very little of Apple Tom after that first day. The vet had drawn an abscessed tooth from the little gelding, and every day the gypsy and his son would harness it up to the flat cart and scour the surrounding farms and villages for scrap. At night

Roddy sorted the scrap over, carefully removing the non-ferrous content and piling the rest alongside the vardo. The tangled heap of metal grew daily.

They returned one afternoon with a pony plough on the cart and drove straight into the yard with it.

'Just right for your gallower, you could turn a bit of ground over with this,' said Apple Tom, sitting on the cart swinging his legs.

He wanted fifteen pounds for it. I offered ten. Roddy joined in the bargaining: 'We can scrap it for more than that, mister.' I doubted this and refused to up my offer. He had had a good deal over the clothes and I was determined to show him I could be as hard as he was. Apple Tom rolled a cigarette, carefully tamping the loose bits of tobacco with a brown forefinger. 'We'll split the difference; twelve and a half.'

I shook my head. 'It is worth ten to me and no more.'

They were in no hurry. Man and boy settled themselves comfortably on the cart; they sat silent for a moment, then started the sales talk. The plough was 'rare, a good 'un, complete, handled nicely, not worn, a bonny 'un, sturdy, well made', and, considering its covering of rust, surprisingly, 'like new'.

I walked over to the cart and examined the plough carefully. 'It's the best I have ever seen.' Both gypsies brightened. 'I normally give six to eight quid for them, but this one is a beauty and, like I said, I'll give a tenner for it. If that's any good to you, shove it under the barn.' I turned and walked into the kitchen.

From my chair by the fire I watched them back the pony and cart under the barn and lift off the plough.

Roddy was soon at the back door. 'It's safe under the barn, mister, we've sheeted it up. That'll be a tenner, mister.' Vicky had been baking and trays of buns stood on the table, cooling.

Roddy grinned cheekily. 'Them buns smell nice, missus; we never get buns.' He left with a ten-pound note in one hand and two warm buns in the other.

Roddy worked hard for a small boy. He cared for the horses, rabbited and sorted scrap. He aped his father in every way and could adopt the same old-world courtesy when it suited him. Roddy talked a lot about his father, but never mentioned his mother. She had not been born to the travelling life, marrying Apple Tom while he was doing National Service. She must have been quite pretty in her youth, but she had aged prematurely and seemed to have a sad life. Her days were spent either in the vardo or in Nellie May's cottage. Roddy did what little shopping they required. The woman seemed to wash clothes every day. If it was fine they were spread over the gorse bushes to dry and if it was wet they hung limply under the tarpaulin which stretched from one side of the vardo.

The children had just left for school when Roddy knocked at the back door. 'Them buns were smashing, mister. We never get buns.'

I handed him two more buns and made to shut the door. He stepped forward and pressed his thin body against the jamb. 'Them clothes you sold me dad are smashin'! They're good warm clothes and they fits smashin'.' The cheeky, ingratiating grin spread across his face. 'You wouldn't be havin' a tie to go with them, would you, mister?'

He crammed a bun into his mouth and followed me through the kitchen into the hallway where the clothes lay. I was a bit out of patience and grabbed the first tie I came upon. It was navy blue with a light blue stripe; should go well enough with the grey pinstripe, I thought, as Roddy hurried off with it.

One thing that had puzzled us was how Apple Tom was

going to cope with the enormous pile of scrap iron he had acquired. This became apparent when two of his fellow travellers arrived with a large wagon. The iron was bargained for *en masse*, but the brass and copper were weighed carefully before being bagged and hoisted on to the wagon. It was a sure sign that the gypsies were about to move. The wiser gardeners in the village looked over their crops and harvested anything that was of reasonable size. Better a half-grown turnip than no turnip at all.

The following morning I counted the ducks carefully. All seemed well. I could hear the jingle of harness as the big skewball was backed between the shafts of the vardo. Apple Tom, immaculate in his new clothes, led the mare off the common and down through the village. The little gelding was tied to the back of the vardo and the woman and the boy walked alongside. Vicky and I stood in the lounge window and watched them pass.

The Colonel stood at the gate, his labrador by his side.

Apple Tom raised his hat with a flamboyant sweep of his hand. 'Mornin', General.'

The Colonel stood expressionless. Two of his Silver Appleyard ducks were missing.

That night in The Ship everyone was talking of the gypsies and everyone commented on the smartness of Apple Tom. Where had he got those clothes? I was on the point of enlightening them when I noticed the Colonel staring at me from his corner seat.

'What I'd like to know,' he boomed, 'is where did the bounder get that Old Etonian tie?'

I grabbed my beer and almost fell down the two steps into the taproom.

Chapter 15

The wheelwright's shop and the blacksmith's stand next door to each other at the bottom of the village green. The blacksmith's is now a joiner's shop, but the wheelwright's stands silent and neglected. When her father died, Mrs Thompson turned the key in the lock and left the workshop to moulder for two decades. When we built our coup cart, we acquired a pair of wheels and an axle from Long John and made the body from exterior plywood screwed on to an elm frame. The shafts we fashioned from steel tubing, welding on brackets and bolting them to the body. When the cart was finished and painted it looked really well, with the exception of the shafts. They were cumbersome and ugly, and yawed from side to side as Topic walked. What we needed was a pair of ash shafts steamed to narrow on to the pony's body.

I peered through the grimed windows of the wheelwright's. There were six or eight pairs of shafts hanging from the roof. Would they be sound after all these years or would they be riddled with woodworm and, more to the point, would

Mrs Thompson be willing to sell us a pair? She was an aunt of Baz's so we asked him to approach her on our behalf. The old lady thought about it for a day or two. Baz brought the message back: yes, she would sell us a pair of shafts.

The key grated in the lock, sending a little stream of powdered rust to the ground. Baz had to force the door open against an accumulated growth of weed and grass. The workshop was dark and musty, a thick layer of grey dust covered everything. We dropped the shafts to the floor and backed off as they shed a cloud of dust which made us cough. They were sound, just one or two wormholes in the ones which had been stacked on the outside. We matched up a pair of the smaller ones and threw them out on to the village green. Baz tapped the racks of elm blanks; bored through and roughed out with the axe, they waited for the silent lathe.

'I helped him cut these. We cut them from an elm we dropped in Ted's. Bloody hard work – it wor like cuttin' iron – but they make the best nafs, these from the bottom of the tree.' The gnarled hand patted the dusty blanks.

A pile of roughed-out felloes was stacked like a Chinese pagoda and spokes stood ranked in sizes against the length of one wall. A half-finished wheel lay on the stool, its stiff spokes shaped and tenoned, its turned naf iron banded and bushed ready for the axle it would never see. Ramsthwaite carts had had a good name. Ted had one rotting away in the corner of his orchard; the ironwork was well smithed and the bed frames and panel edges were chamfered and scalloped to give a little touch of finesse to this most mundane of vehicles.

The coup cart was essentially a coup on wheels. The coup was a rectangular box on sledge runners, used on the high fell and steeply sloping fields where wheeled carts were impractical.

The sturdy dales ponies dragged them up to the moortop filled with stone for walling and brought them down laden with bracken for bedding. Sometimes, when a loaded cart had to be brought down a steep track, a coup laden with stones or peat would be dragged behind to act as a brake.

The wheelwright has always earned his bread hard. Oak and elm are not the easiest of woods to work and with every mortice hand-cut and every spoke formed with drawknife and spokeshave it was a good man who could make and tyre a wheel in two days. With the coming of the railways, mass-produced Scotch carts from Birmingham chugged north, chained three at a time on to the big flat trucks, to close the door of many a wheelwright's shop. A team of three men with steam-powered bandsaws and lathes, setting the work out with jigs and formers, could make ten wheels in a day. The mass-produced carts were sound, well-made vehicles but they were too unstable for the dales and the hill farmers clung steadfastly to their low-slung coup carts, even after the little grey Ferguson tractors had ousted the horse. They merely cut off the shafts and welded a tow bar in place.

The yard at the back of the shop was grown high with elder. Dried nettles thrust through the racks of elm and oak boards. The tyring ring, set on a plinth of cobbles, was heavy with rust and tiny clumps of wall-pepper peeped from the cracks in the huge stone trough. The yard was closed in on all four sides and had slept for twenty years. Only the marauding cat had disturbed its tranquillity.

We carried the shafts home and set about them with plane and sandpaper. 'Hard as the Devil's forehead,' muttered Baz, as the plane refused to bite.

Bundling them into the van, we set off for the Radfords. Richard had a belt sander which disciplined the hardest of woods. They cleaned up to a pale beige, the long grain following the steamed curves. The figuring was so pleasing for ash that, had we not painted the cart, I would merely have varnished them. They had to be set high on the cart to suit Topic's fourteen hands, but they improved its appearance enormously.

Mrs Thompson had never said how much she wanted for the shafts, so Baz was dispatched once more.

'She'd like that little pot sheep, if that's all right.'

I peeled the price ticket off the eighteenth-century Staffordshire sheep and wrapped it carefully in tissue paper. The shafts had cost me more than the rest of the cart put together.

Baz turned the package in his hands. 'There's a pair of wheels with all the springing and ironwork to make a Wensleydale shandry in there.'

I looked at our stock of Staffordshire figures and shook my head. 'I don't think I could afford it yet, Baz.'

The new shafts suited Topic much better. We started to work her more around the holding, and one evening we spruced her up and used the cart to deliver a set of balloon-back chairs to Lalbeck.

Coming back, we set a board across the cart for a seat and the whole family managed to squeeze on to it. Topic threw her neck into the collar and trotted up the village green with her happy load.

Old Mr Hall waved from the wash-fold. 'Yer look like a row of sparrers coming home.'

Bullpen Farm had, in the past, been one of the biggest holdings in the village; all the land that Ted farmed had once belonged to it along with the forty sheep gaits on the moor, which had been retained by the Estate, together with the shooting rights.

The holding still carried with it obligatory membership of the Altondale Drainage Board and rights of turbary on the moor. Whenever the price of coal rose, it would be followed by muttered threats in The Ship to 'get up on the tops and cut a few turves'. Ted told us that the last peat had been cut during the war, when it had been hawked around the village at five shillings a load, dried and stacked.

We decided to exercise our rights and fetch a load of peat off the tops before winter set in. Topic was working well in gears. She was fit and strong, and could pull half a ton of logs up Drover's Lane without showing any undue strain. We had no doubt she could have pulled the little coup cart to the top of the moor, but we were worried about the descent. With no brakes and the rough track precluding the use of a roller scotch, she would not have been able to hold even the empty cart back on the breechings. Ted, as always, came to the rescue. He had a set of panniers which had been used for carrying a pair of back-cans. We let out the belly-band to take Topic's fat girth, and lashed two wicker baskets on to the pannier steps. All we needed now was a proper peat spade. Long John had several.

'Where are you cutting?' he asked, and pulled a face when I told him. 'It's poor stuff up there.'

Poor stuff or not, it was free to us for the taking, and we were determined to try it. I put a hemp halter with a long lead rein on Topic and slung the panniers across her broad back. She had an annoying habit of blowing her belly out whenever we attempted to fasten a girth tightly, so I left her stood in the yard, the pannier straps dangling in the mud, as I went to help Vicky with the sandwiches and flasks of soup.

There was no warmth in the weak sun, but soon we were opening our coats and breathing heavily, as we climbed the steep track to the tops. Topic ambled along behind, the vacuum flasks rolling from side to side in her offside pannier. The two dogs scampered ahead of us; excited by the smells of the moor they plunged in and out of the heather, their brown and white rumps wagging incessantly. I carried the peat spade over my shoulder. I had filed the blade sharp and straightened the wing. Ted said that in the old days, when they had come down from a stint of cutting, you could see to shave yourself in the spades, so polished were they.

The old diggings were easy to find, and we sank down on the springy heather beside one to regain our breath before we made a start. Behind us the pale smoky outline of the lakeland hills could just be seen, while in front the green dale stretched out towards the Plain of York. It was a solitary place, the haunt of curlew, sheep and grouse.

I squared the old face of the digging, throwing the moss-faced turves into its centre. I had to stand in the digging to clear the rough grass from the top. The wet peat sank under my boots, every footprint filling with dark-brown water as soon as the foot was lifted. We squatted behind an old shooting butt and ate our simple lunch, before we set to work cutting the clean turves.

I pitched the turves on to the banking to drain and, although a chill breeze played about the moortop, I soon had to doff coat and cap for it was warm work. Cutting the turves square and regular was not as easy as I had thought it would be. When I had cut enough to fill both panniers, we lay back in the heather and finished the soup. It was so peaceful on the moortop. The only sounds were the bleating of a lonely sheep and the steady panting of the dogs. Topic nuzzled amongst the heather. I had taken off the panniers and tethered her to a bunch of ling, but she had soon pulled free. She showed no inclination for making off, so we left her to nose her way around our little encampment. She sniffed the turves and got the crusts from our sandwiches, much to the disgust of the dogs.

We had brought no watch with us and were well out of earshot of the bells of any church. The sun was low in the sky and it must have been well into the afternoon when I caught Topic and hoisted the panniers across her back. We stacked the turves carefully into the wicker baskets, for they were quite fragile. Topic did not seem at all put out by her new role of packhorse. Brown, peaty water dripped from each pannier as we made our way steadily down the track. We stacked the turves carefully under the Dutch barn, staggering the layers so the wind could blow through them.

Ted viewed them critically. 'A bit springy – fast burners.' He leaned on Topic's fat rump. The pony shifted the weight on her rear leg to favour the one nearest to him. 'When I wor a lad, t'owd fellah used to send me out to t'peathouse for six turves. They were stacked on t'fire after we were through milking, and when they were burnt away it wor bedtime. I used to spend a lot o'time looking for t'six biggest.'

Topic went to the manger readily; her day out on the moor had sharpened her appetite. No lazy picking and nuzzling out the horse cubes tonight – she set to work with a will. Whenever we worked her I always gave her a good measure, and trailed a pattern of molasses over her feed before letting her to it. She stood stock still, her prominent jaw muscles working, as I pulled the panniers off her back and rubbed her down with a straw wisp. She was none the worse for her labours – wet patches on her flanks from the peat water and the tangled and soaked feather on her legs were the only signs that she had done a day's work.

I had been worried that the panniers would gall her flanks,

but they had been made by men who knew the shape of the Dales pony. The straw-stuffed pads had distributed the weight along the bank of muscle which lined each side of her spine, and the broad breast band and breechings had seen to it that the wicker baskets had hardly moved, even when we had tackled the steepest of tracks.

Vicky and I were thoroughly tired by our day on the 'tops' and, as soon as the children were home from school, we built up the fire, cooked the evening meal and settled ourselves in for the night.

A Yorkshire broad-arm is a good chair for aching bones. With its deep-shaped saddle and well-raked back, its arms are placed just right for a tired man to hold a mug of tea in one hand and a good pipe in the other. With slippered feet thrust into the hearth and the tobacco jar not too far away, a man soon falls to day-dreaming. The cares and worries of the day ebb away and a delicious warmth creeps over his limbs, and it is not long before his head starts to droop gently to his chest. It is at this moment that a caring wife will ease the mug and pipe from the relaxing hands and 'shush' the children.

Vicky did not get to the shushing bit, for Peter burst in from the hallway, one of Canary Mary's notelets in his hand. She must have called while we were on the moor.

'Aunty Mary's got an ex-ve-one-one kist for you, and she says it's nice.'

Slippered feet and aching bones are enemies of action, but the thought of the Chippendale silver table standing sadly in the corner of the wash-house in its pale undercoat brought me to my feet.

'Come on, Vicky, let's get down there before she paints the bugger.'

Chapter 16

We are quite successful at breeding ducks. Our Khaki Campbells lay like machines, our Muscovys wax fat and our little Silver Appleyards lie on the banking and look beautiful. The children will not eat duck eggs and Vicky finds them poor for cooking, but they have a ready market among the villagers. Ted's wife sticks her head around the door. 'Any duck eggs?' The coins chink into the cracked tureen, and so the laying ducks subsidize the ones for the pot.

If we were interested in the pure economics of duck ownership we would undoubtedly keep Aylesburys for fattening – they are quicker to mature and put a good depth of flesh on their broad breasts – but once you have tasted young Muscovy, roasted slowly in a wood-fired oven and liberally basted with cider, all other waterfowl pale in comparison. A tender young guinea-fowl with chestnut stuffing, strips of home-cured bacon sliced into its breast, set on a bed of asparagus and hemmed around with small new potatoes rolled in butter and sprinkled with freshly chopped mint can, on occasions, come near to equalling the dark, brown, dry, almost gamey, flesh of the Muscovy.

It is, as the Iron Duke once said, 'a near-run thing'. Some will have it that the young Muscovy is really a goose and not a duck, but whatever species that magnificent bird graces, it certainly is in a class of its own when brought to the table, garlanded with watercress and crisps and the steaming jug of cider gravy set alongside it. The very thought of it can make one long for a cold, gusty winter's night and a kitchen warm with crackling logs and filled with the delicious aroma of a roasting Muscovy. With a good bottle of Rioja, well decanted and breathing its sunniness into the air, sitting on the dresser next to a blue Wensleydale; the dogs sleeping fitfully under the table and the cat curling a marmalade tail around soft paws and staring unblinking into the fire. Slippered feet scrubbing lazily on the hearth and the big meerschaum pipe sitting by the tobacco jar on the mantelpiece, a taper laid alongside it ready for when the Windsor chairs are pulled from the table and set once again each side of the fireplace. On a night like that, the glories of Versailles could not tempt me from my humble Dales farmhouse.

If we are to have our winter of content, we must have our glorious summer of productivity. The potatoes have to be hoed, the peas sticked and the clutches of eggs watched over. Muscovys have a reputation for being bad sitters but our flock, when left to its own devices, manages to bring off two broods a year. The cache of eggs, secreted in the deep straw of the Dutch barn, will grow daily until there are ten, twelve or even fourteen. This is the time they have to be watched carefully, for the duck may refuse to go broody and abandon the nest. Then comes a frantic search round the village for a broody hen.

'Have you a broody hen, Colonel?'

The Colonel guards his broodies jealously, for he, too, has the same problem. 'Try Rabbit. His Buff Orpingtons are always broody.'

If the duck sits she is immovable, and once ensconced will defy all comers until the little black-billed, brown-and-yellow-banded ducklings break from their shell. We are lucky to have running water at hand, for when the duck leaves the nest to feed, usually in the late evening, she will wade into the stream and go through a cleansing ritual. She returns to her nest wet, and so saves us the task of sprinkling the eggs. Muscovys are very fertile – if she sits on a dozen eggs, we get a dozen duck-lings. The problem of Muscovy husbandry is in the rearing. Good, tenacious mothers that they are, they tend to rove too far during the day and the ducklings become worn out. If it is a hot, sunny day they are prone to heat exhaustion, and any stragglers that get separated from the little wandering tribe have a thousand enemies – rooks, rats, magpies, cats, dogs and that new menace, the mink, all find the tiny fluffy balls of duckling delectable.

We have learned our lesson. We have built two temporary pens which cross the beck at its widest part, and have a pas-sageway between them. Each duck is content and safe with her brood, and the proud drake parades between the pens giving his care and advice to each family in turn. Ducks grow at an astonishing rate; no bigger than a plum when hatched, in a month's time they are the size of a partridge, three months and except for a little difference in the plumage they are indistin-guishable from their parents.

Mine were at the partridge stage when disaster struck. Peter had taken on the job of assistant duck-keeper. He was thorough in the execution of his duties: the troughs were kept clean, the grit boxes topped up, the tattiest of the vegetables were hurled into the pens each day and the feeding was regular and sound.

Temporary pens have temporary doors, usually fastened with billy-band, and it is my belief that the assistant duck-keeper should, at frequent intervals, inspect the billy-band hinges. Perhaps we thrust great responsibility on to the young shoulders too early. The sad outcome, however, was that early one morning, as I whistled my way across the yard, cheerfully swinging my milkcan, I noticed the door of one of the pens was lying flat in the grass, frayed bits of billy-band wafting mockingly from the gatepost. Duck and brood were gone – a good mature Muscovy and ten partridge-sized ducklings, just beginning to soft feather on their breasts and putting out the first pens on their stubby wings.

I still had a brood of nine safely penned, and it may be thought that greed gave birth to the grief until it is explained to the uninitiated the bargaining power one holds when one has an oven-ready Muscovy in one's gifting. Ted will mow two acres of thistles for one and the Lewises will smile and push one of their best cheeses across the counter. Richard Radford will have a new bow on the Windsor chair for Saturday and tickets for two of the best seats in Lalbeck's tiny theatre on the opening night of *The Pirates of Penzance* present no problem.

I knew the ducks would be downstream somewhere, so I called the dogs and set off down the beck. Rabbit was sat in the hedgebottom at the top of Drover's Lane, one of his best sticks between his knees and a terrier at each side of him.

'They're on the mill dam,' he called without taking the stalk of grass from his mouth.

The dogs plunged straight into the dam, sending the duck and ducklings surging, white-waked, into the reeds.

Muscovys do not quack, they have a peculiar hissing call, and the reeds shook and vibrated to hisses as the family re-formed, safe among the tall stalks. I called the dogs out and tested the bed of the dam with my stick. It pushed easily into the mud bottom until the handle touched the water. Even with waders, I would not be able to get across to the ducks. They had gone quiet, and only a few hisses came from the reeds as I scattered the bread I had brought on to the water – no sense in letting them get thin, the dam had a stable population of moorhens and another eleven beaks feeding from it must stretch the food supply.

I sat on the bank and considered my problem. The bed of tall reedmace, forty feet from either banking, was grown around with dark-hair crowfoot and ivy duckweed. Old reeds, broken and brown with age, had been trodden into narrow runways by the moorhens who nested in the centre of the bed. The Muscovys had completely ousted the poor moorhens, who chinked in and out of the sweet flag by the mill leat. Deposed from their citadel, they were restless and easily put to flight. The dogs sent them scrambling over the stone parapet to plunge fat-bodied into the wheelrun. As long as the ducks were in the reeds I was helpless. I had to get them on to the banking and drive them away from the water.

It seemed there were two courses open to me. I could either flush them from the reedbed or I could tempt them on to the banking with food. I would try the temptation. I went back home and fetched their trough, along with half a bucketful of wheat. I would feed them every day, each time moving the trough further away from the dam. Once they were far enough from the water, I could charge in and drive them home in triumph.

Every morning for six days I trudged down to the dam with my bucket of wheat. The ducks soon became used to the routine and would come surging across the water to feed, but no matter how hard I tried I could not get them away from the dam. When I judged they were fully occupied eating, I ran as fast as I could down the banking, whooping and shouting and waving my stick, but every time they beat me to the water. I tried sneaking up on them, but they seemed to feel the very gentlest of footfalls on the banking. They would raise their heads and silently twist them until twenty-two coal-black beads stared at me. The old duck would hiss her alarm and, in a flurry of feathers and slapping of webbed feet, they would stream off in a wide arc and plunge back into the water. If I set the trough a long way from the dam's edge they would refuse to feed until I had withdrawn to the top of the dam, where the beck fell into it over a little weir.

I got much advice from the taproom gang. Ted suggested I leave them on the dam until Christmas, and then we could go down and shoot them.

The Colonel plumped for dogs. 'A good old curly coat would have them off that reedbed in no time.' The trouble is, no one keeps curly-coated retrievers any more.

Charlie gave considerable thought to my problem as he leaned on the bar at lunchtimes. 'Take the drake down and tether him on the banking – the duck has been away from him so long now, she'll be aching for a bit of "rumpty-tumpty". When they're at it, pounce on 'em; if you lead the duck away the young 'uns will follow.'

Sound though the scheme seemed, Charlie was not up on

duck psychology. The drake was ignored and, much to my chagrin, broke loose and joined the errant family. I now had a round dozen Muscovys loose on the dam.

Miss Denholm's letter to the Estate was beautifully written on quality paper. It listed her many qualifications, told of her desire to conserve all that was worth conserving, and asked for permission to survey the mill.

The Estate replied with begrudging agreement. They were, as they put it, 'pestered to death about the mill'.

Miss Denholm had had a sheltered upbringing. Her parents were both of the old order, almost Victorian, and the girl's education had been thorough and successful. She held a first-class honours degree and had a career in local government, which provided her with a good living – enough, in fact, for her to buy a cottage of her own and run a prestige sports car. She was thirty-five years of age and, although she had had 'her chances', Mr Right had yet to appear.

I sat on the banking watching her unload her gear from the car. Baz had made a proud boast in The Ship the night before:

'Tha's buggered about long enough wi' them ducks. I'll come down and git 'em for thee tomorrow night.'

Miss Denholm had equipped herself with all that a good industrial archaeologist needs. I watched her carry wholewheat biscuits, pens, pencils, pads, a splendid tape measure which ingeniously fixed itself to the walls so that she could measure buildings single-handed, a tartan car-rug and a Polaroid camera. She also had a pole, two metres long and graduated in metric and imperial. The good lady had discovered what all field workers discover, that single-handed mensuration is always difficult and sometimes impossible. Long winter evenings in the

164

cottage had been spent training herself to judge sizes. She developed this skill to a high degree and it stood her in good stead when she made her forays into the field.

I could see her moving about the mill, through a small paneless window set alongside the wheel. The window was two feet above the stone parapet and had been constructed to give the miller a lookout over the dam. Without leaving his station at the jiggler, he could keep an eye on the leat and the head of water he had. Miss Denholm had donned a blue nylon overall with an elasticated waistband, pulled back her long blonde hair and tied it with a ribbon. It gave her a girlish look, for she had the soft delicate complexion that only comes with good living. Nuns have such complexions.

The ducks were settled quietly to the reedbed, a pied wagtail sat on the sluice and dipped his tail in a friendly way. It was a beautiful evening, warm and still; a soft mist lay over the meadows and the sun, a full, rich glorious sun, fell slowly behind Fox Covert, throwing the trees into black silhouette and sending long fingers of shadow to reach out and touch the browsing rabbits.

I had almost given up on Baz when I heard his heavy boots scrunching down the lane. He was wearing a blue sweatshirt and a pair of khaki shorts which reached down to his knees, and on his head he was carrying an enormous zinc bath we had got from a house clearance.

His voice boomed from under the bath. 'Make way for the Ramsthwaite man o' war, Cap-tin Baz in command.'

I launched the bath. 'God bless her and all who sail in her.'

Baz removed his boots and climbed in. He knelt in a crouching position and, with a stout stick thrusting from the prow, he dipped his huge hands into the water and paddled his craft across to the reedbed. The ducks were unmoved. Baz hollered and shouted and poked his stick into their island refuge, to no avail.

In exasperation, he stood up in the bath and laid his stick vigorously about the reeds. It was his undoing. Any naval architect will tell you that a flat-bottomed craft with a high centre of gravity will soon lose its stability. Baz plunged into the water and sent a wave sweeping over the little runways of the reedbed, which in turn sent the ducks hissing and splashing across the dam. Baz surfaced, his hair full of duckweed, and struck out towards the mill. He climbed out on to the stone parapet, the green water streaming from him. The khaki shorts followed the sweatshirt on to the stones as Baz picked the duckweed from his wet body.

Miss Denholm had been drawn to the window by the noise and now she moved back into the shadows as Baz's naked body filled her view. Her expertise at judging size told her that he was over six feet tall, but modesty forbade that she should apply her skill to any specific part of his anatomy, although she was quick to register that he was indeed a well-built young man.

Her genteel upbringing had instilled in her a caring for her fellow beings, so with a polite cough, and averting her eyes, she pushed the tartan car-rug through the window. Baz never turned a hair. He thanked her politely and draped the rug around his shoulders, pinching the front together with one hand. Miss Denholm offered hot coffee and Baz sat noisily on the stone, saluting the lady with his free hand before taking the flask-top.

I gathered Baz's boots and dropped them on to the stone parapet beside him. 'I'll fetch the van down, Baz, and take you home.'

Baz waved me away with a wink. 'I'm all right. You go and mek sure them other ducks is still at home.'

I looked back from the top of the lane. Miss Denholm had joined Baz on the stone parapet, they were both leaning forward, swinging their legs over the mill leat, and their heads were close together in the manner people adopt when they are discussing industrial archaeology.

The following morning, instead of taking the dogs down Drover's Lane I turned up the moor road and walked along by the council houses and across the common towards Baz's cottage. I had no ulterior motive; merely a wish to enquire after the health of the intrepid sailor. Vicky had seen the little red sports car speed up the moor road at a quarter to midnight, the splendid tartan-clad figure of Baz erect in the passenger seat.

The car was parked outside the cottage. During the night we had had an hour of gentle rain, the kind of rain that falls vertically but softly and leaves dry patches under the cabbages. No one had put the hood up on the car and the tonneau cover was folded on the narrow back seat. The clipboard and pads lay soaking wet in the foot-well of the passenger seat and the ingenious tape measure was thrust into the glove compartment along with one of Baz's boots. Baz was normally an early riser but all the curtains were drawn in the cottage. I had no wish to pry so I retraced my steps.

Ted was leaning on the gate, his chin resting on his bare arms. He grinned. 'Looks like the lass wor looked after better than her motor last night.'

Baz made a vain attempt to quell the village gossips. 'I merely offered the woman bed and breakfast.' Baz owned one knife, one fork, two spoons, one tin mug and one single bed. Whatever his spartan establishment lacked in facilities he must have made up for in personal attention, for when Miss Denholm finally emerged to fling her bag into the back of the little car and gunned it down through the village, there was not a happier-looking woman in England.

Billy Potts was Ted's cousin. They were very similar and were often mistaken for each other, but one infallible way of recognizing Billy was by his wellingtons. They were always black and he cut the top three inches from the legs so they flobbled against his muscular calves. He wore them day in and day out, summer and winter alike. One summer's night, when Billy had been haytiming late and called in at the taproom to wash the dust from his tonsils, Rabbit's vigorous shuffling of the dominoes had sent one plummeting down one of Billy's wellies. The thick hand, fingers working feverishly, had failed to retrieve it, so Billy had taken the boot off. The resulting stench had sent the drinkers flying to the door for air. Rabbit thrust his head through the serving hatch and pleaded with Charlie for some kind of spray to kill the evil cloud of bacteria he swore was rising from Billy's stockinged foot.

Billy slapped the domino on the table, pulled his boot back on and took a drink from each of the glasses the drinkers had abandoned. 'You can come back to the trenches now, lads; the gas attack is over.'

Baz fetched the damp cloth which always hung alongside the dartboard and carefully wiped the double five before returning it to the pack.

Billy didn't frequent the pub often. Although he was very wealthy, he did not believe in spending his money. He travelled up to the Scottish borders and down to the Welsh marches on his cattle-dealing trips, and usually it was either a particularly successful deal or an unbearably hot night which brought him into the taproom. He would stand with his back to the fireplace and, when sufficient beer had been gulped down his turkey-red gullet, he would break into song.

'I'm Billy Potts of Altonshotts, I've yows as big as cows – an' cows as big as elephants.'

This night was not hot and Billy had had no successful deal – he had heard about my ducks. 'Tell thee what I'll do. For two young 'uns, when they're ready to eat that is, I'll ketch all the ducks.'

Two young ones! That was typical of Billy. I hesitated before replying.

Billy put his hand on my shoulder and thrust his face close to me. 'The mink are comin' up the beck and if they git among t'ducks th'ar buggered.'

I had heard that the mink had taken a lot of Totty Brown's ducks and that they were playing havoc with the wild mallard on the Estate. 'OK, Billy, two – but you pluck and dress them.'

Billy nodded his agreement and put his empty glass into my hand. 'We'll just 'ave a little drink to settle the deal.'

Billy pushed the big brass horn with the black rubber bulb into my hands; his instructions were clear and concise.

'Hide yoursen' in the long grass, and after a bit give big honks until the ducks show interest, then a little honk now and then when I start me callin'. When the ducks are in the back of the wagon, sneak down t'other side of the wall and pull the rope.'

Billy backed his wagon opposite the mill door and dropped the tailgate. He clipped a wire frame across the wagon back and, raising it three feet, he supported it with a stick. A thin rope was tied around the stick and passed over the wall into Totty's garth. Billy then scrambled under the frame and hid himself in a pile of straw at the front end of the wagon.

I started to honk, big honks as instructed. Billy's arm emerged from the pile of straw and gave me a thumbs-up signal. Honkers respond to encouragement and I worked the black bulb vigorously. It had a disturbing effect on the wildlife of the dam. All the birds stopped singing, the nervous moorhens scrambled up the stone parapet and threw themselves frantically into the wheelrun, the ducks raised their heads in alarm and scuttled from the reedbed to swim round and round, their heads stabbing forward in an agitated way.

I decided the ducks had now shown interest and stopped honking. Billy gave me another thumbs up and started his calling. It was a low, piercing whistle of three or four seconds, followed by a peculiar trilling sound he achieved by blowing through a little pool of saliva he gathered in the gap between his front teeth.

It had a marked effect on the ducks. The little flotilla stopped swimming and rode silently at anchor. Three times Billy called, and then I honked. At the honk the ducks became a little agitated and moved nearer the banking. Three more calls, a little honk and nearer still to the banking. My admiration for Billy grew. With calls and honks we soon had all the ducks on the banking and making their way towards the mill and Billy's wagon, when a large barn owl swooped from the mill roof on soft outstretched wings and alighted on the tailgate. It swivelled its head to stare wide-eyed at the pile of straw. The ducks stopped in their tracks. No amount of calling or honking would entice them any further. Billy's hand thrust from the straw and wagged towards the owl.

'Piss off, go on, piss off.' The owl stared at him, unblinking. 'Pee-ss off,' Billy shouted.

The more the owl stared the louder Billy shouted. I remembered the effect the honking had had on the birdlife so I pumped the bulb as hard as I could. The owl rose lazily, its huge soft brown wings carrying it noiselessly back to the mill roof. Billy resumed the calling, I gave the requisite low honks and the ducks resumed their steady march towards the tailgate. It was time for my flanking manoeuvre. I crawled across the lane, climbed the wall into the garth and ran to where Billy had jammed the rope in the wall toppings. As soon as the ducks waddled under the wire frame I gave a hefty tug on the rope. The frame dropped behind a dozen frantic ducks.

Billy climbed out of the wagon back; he was covered in straw and his grin stretched from ear to ear. 'Told thi, told thi,' was all he could say as we bumped up the lane.

Vicky brought out two mugs of coffee for the duck catchers as we sat on the apple house steps and watched Peter and Sally carry the birds one by one back to their pen.

Billy's cattle wagon was brand new. It was brush-painted fire engine red. Several bristles were embedded on the door and curtains of paint drooped across the front. Billy saw me looking at it.

'I git 'em in primer and paint 'em missen', it saves a lot of brass.' Billy sucked in a mouthful of coffee; he gave his long whistle and the short trill. Both pens of Muscovys stood stock still. Billy laughed and climbed into the cab. 'Ev to be off, I'm goin' up to Dave Newman to fetch the last of his milk beasts. He's comin' off.'

Dave and Ann Newman had taken a holding at the top of Robins Ghyll. It was a wild, lonely spot and the views from the seventeenth-century farmhouse were stunning. A wild expanse of moorland poured itself into the valley in front of the house in a series of velvet folds, and then rose in a gentle, green, swelling hill straining under a net of walls. It was the haunt of merlin and stonechat, a beautiful, unspoilt place. I told Billy I couldn't imagine anyone leaving a place like that.

Billy started the engine and sucked his teeth. 'Aye, but ye ev to make a living. Yer can't eat the scenery.'

Chapter 17

The Colonel is adamant, The Ship is a corruption of 'The Sheep'. As we are thirty miles from the nearest navigable water, and locally ewes become yows and hams become hames, he could be right. The pub is the centre of village social life. Unchanged structurally for over a century and not feeling the decorator's brush too frequently, its nicotine-yellowed walls and ceilings give it a seedy look in broad daylight, but when night falls and the red-shaded lamps cast their arcs of warm light and a fire crackles in the grate, it has an inviting homeliness. Often a villager says, 'I'll just have an hour', or, 'I'll just nip in for one', finally to emerge in the small hours of the next day to go home sheepishly to an irate wife.

The antique trade has its window stoppers; Charlie has his warm lights winking invitingly through mock leaded windows. The wall-lights, red plush panels alternating with coaching scenes, highlight the polished brass and copper. Viewed from outside on a rain-sodden winter's evening, the effect is seductive. Charlie knows this. In winter he never draws the curtains until ten o'clock. Many a car squeals to a halt, clunks into reverse and whines back to the unmade car-park.

Charlie is a good landlord. A big, quietly spoken man from the steel mills of Tyneside, his life's ambition had been to run a country pub and to Charlie the reality is as good as the dream. He works hard and every opening time when he draws the heavy bolt on the front door and, no matter what the weather, swings it wide open, the copper-topped bar gleams and every ashtray stands clean and empty on its shining Britannia table, surrounded by equally spaced beer-mats.

Charlie is a great diplomat; he never voices any strong opinions on politics, religion or horseracing and, although he is a clever poker player, he can never be enticed into one of the tap-room games.

'Play wi' you buggers? My brass doesn't come that easy.'

'You ought to share it out a bit,' jokes Rabbit, but Charlie is not to be drawn.

The only subject he can really get heated up about is cricket; he is a fanatical follower of Yorkshire's fortunes. Ted pulls his leg mercilessly.

'You shouldn't be supporting Yorkshire, you haven't lived here long enough.'

Charlie just smiles, pours himself another bottle and stares at his cherished collection of horsebrasses. He and his wife have never had a holiday together since they took over The Ship ten years ago. Ethel visits her sister in Whitby for a week and Charlie makes several pilgrimages to Headingley during the season.

The Ship has good, deep cellars with vaulted roofs. They are whitewashed annually and their stone-flagged floors scrubbed weekly. They hardly vary a degree in temperature over the year.

Charlie pulls salt-water through the pumps daily and washes everything religiously with the correct solution of disinfectant, but for all his dedicated cellarwork, he fails to put on a good pint. Ted refers to it politely as sludge, but Rabbit bangs his empty glass on the taproom hatch and cheerfully calls for another pint of 'witch piss'.

Charlie ignores them both. He pours himself another bottle and consoles himself that he does everything possible. 'It's the brewery; they send me the tailings.'

The lounge is the heart of the pub. With its two sets of hand pumps, the nickel plating worn from their finials, and the big arched fireplace, which in winter draws one like a magnet, it is the hub of the village. Market day in Lalbeck fills it with farmers and cattle dealers, and the Parish Council stand around the fireplace and settle weighty matters before they mount the steps to the long room to open the meeting. Several coaching prints hang on the walls and Charlie's collection of horsebrasses is nailed firmly to the beams. Ethel fetches her tall stool and polishes them every Friday. The polish seeps into the beam around each brass and on drying gives it a pale halo.

Over the squat cellar door hangs the famous horned hare of Altondale. A Victorian taxidermist's joke, the moth-eaten head with its tiny horns thrusts, yellow-toothed, from its oak shield. Baz and Rabbit lie in wait on warm summer evenings when the tourists stand and stare at it. They grin at each other and, with practised ease, bait the hook.

'Not many about now.'

'Years since I've seen one.'

The tales vary from felltops awash with battling clans of horned hares, to frightening specimens as big as a dog and afeared of no man. Rabbit will, once the unwary have been ensnared, pull up his trouser leg and show the four-inch-long scar on his left calf. The calloused hand hovers eighteen inches from the floor. 'This big it wor, going like a skoprill, flung me on me back.'

He got the scar trying to push-start a 1920 Enfield motorcycle down Drover's Lane, but such mundane injuries interest no one. Now a horned hare, maddened with lust and enraged at the intervention of a man and his terrier, is quite another story.

The walls of the lounge are lined with pew-like seats; hard-planked backs and bottoms make them very uncomfortable. The rake of the backs is wrong and the little oblongs of edged carpet that Ethel has made for the seats continually break their tape fastenings, as aching bodies shuffle in vain to find a comfortable position.

The taproom is spartan – no edged little oblongs of carpet there. The concrete floor is painted red and the bare lime-washed walls are relieved only by a dartboard, its pockmarked face staring from its wagon tyre surround. Only in the depths of winter will Charlie light a fire in the taproom, for the beer is a penny a pint cheaper in there. The taproom is two steps down from the lounge and the square serving hatch through to the bar is chest high. Charlie keeps the taproom door wedged open. It is covered with notices: darts finals, Leek Club activities and a yellowed poster from the last Altondale Show are upstaged by Rabbit's hand-scrawled advertisement. It is written on a shoe-box lid and stuck on with one drawing pin, 'For sale ferrets'. No name, no address or telephone number, but everyone knows it is Rabbit.

Only rarely do visitors get into the taproom – it looks so cold and bleak – but on a dark winter's night it is the place to be.

The dominoes rattle, a blue fog of smoke rises to the roof, dogs sleep head on paws under the benches and a good bit of 'crack' is to be had. If Rabbit or Baz are on form the laughter wells through the door, drawing smiles or frowns from the lounge clientele. Charlie will bend almost double and thrust his bald head through the hatch, afraid of missing a new tale; the customers can wait.

Rabbit never misses a Thursday night, for it is then that the farmers pay for the odd bit of walling or mole-catching, and it is Thursday nights when the Reverend Murray calls in for the odd glass, after the scout meeting. The Colonel sits on his high stool, blazer-clad elbows firmly planted on the bar, his pipe never leaving his mouth as he nods his agreement with all the good vicar says.

Charlie never keeps to the official closing time. If things are going well in the taproom, he draws the lounge curtains and, leaving Ethel to her tête-à-tête with the Colonel, he descends the two steps with a bottle in each hand.

'It saves trailing,' he says. The Colonel drops the latch behind him as he leaves and it is into the early hours of the next day before the damp grey towel is draped over the pumps.

The highlight of the pub year is the week before Christmas when the Rabbit Clearance Society, the Leek Club and the Altondale Drainage Society all hold their annual dinners in the long room over the lounge. The Goose Club, born out of thrift, has no style; they squander their resources on an annual trip to Blackpool. It is the youngest of the clubs. Formed at the end of the nineteenth century, its members saved pennies throughout the year and sent their officers to the Goose Fairs at Hawes and Reeth to buy the Christmas birds.

Ted's wife comes across to help Ethel cook the dinners. The

food is simple but fit for the gods: huge smiling brown meat and potato pies with jugs of steaming gravy fill the pub with a delicious smell as they are carried up to the long room. The less fortunate watch with envious eyes as the members of the Drainage Society, smart and self-conscious in their dinner jackets, mount the steps.

The beck runs through our land so I am automatically a member. I pay three guineas a year for this privilege. It was my first dinner and I sat next to Ted at the lower table. The big landowners sat at the upper table. The glasses of sherry were passed round, big heavy-bowled sherry glasses almost like Victorian rummers. The sherry was good, first-class stuff. The Reverend Sidney Murray said a short grace and the pies were brought from under their hot towels. Ethel wielded an enormous spoon; sawing through the pie crusts she filled each plate and passed it to Dolly who streamed the heavenly gravy over it.

Ted leaned over to me. 'I only wed her for her gravy.'

Dolly heard him and looked over her glasses at him.

There was little conversation, just the scraping of knives and forks and the clatter of spoons and dishes as Ethel made her way around the table, a pie dish wrapped around with a hessian towel cradled in her arm, the huge spoon hovering. 'Any more?' Dolly followed with the gravy jug.

There were no takers; everyone had had more than enough, for there was gooseberry flan and cream to follow and laid on the sideboard was a magnificent blue Wensleydale cheese. The cheese was one of Mrs Lewis's. It had been turned and watched, patted and thumped and sniffed at until it was perfect. The crust was Van Dyck-brown, thick and crumbly, and the veins of bluey green fanned through the yellowing flesh like ferns. No one wanted to be too full when that cheese thumped on to the table.

Rabbit had been engaged as a waiter for the night. He took what was left of the pies and gravy down to the taproom and mounted the stairs again, banging a huge black japanned tray against his knees. We were not ready for him yet. He leaned against the sideboard and cradled the tray under one arm to hide his activity; the thumb and forefinger of his free hand took a corner from the cheese. Ethel saw him and the heavy spoon caught him on the back of the hand. 'Off! Yer greedy sod.' He grinned and stuffed the cheese into his mouth.

Empty plates were being pushed into the centre of the tables and a polite burp or two showed approval. Ethel's stern look and nod of the head sent Rabbit about his job. He was not skilled in the art of waiting at tables. He slammed the plates on to the tray, crammed the empty jugs with knives and forks and sucked gravy from his calloused thumb.

'Here, Colonel, shove them plates down, owd lad.'

The Colonel shuffled the plates down the table without looking up. Rabbit banged and jangled down the steps as Ethel thwacked great gobs of cream on to the steaming flans. I looked at mine, remembered the cheese and spooned a little from one corner. Ted ate voraciously. He had had more pie than anyone else and now he had more flan. Cream covered his upper lip; his left arm round his plate, protecting, the right one worked his spoon from plate to mouth with clockwork regularity.

The sherry glasses were collected and washed and brought back to the table. Rabbit cleared the last of the plates and Mr Fairbrother crossed to the sideboard and drew the corks from half a dozen bottles of port.

'Should have been decanted,' he complained.

The Colonel leaned back in his chair. 'As long as it's warm, Aubrey.'

The cheese was cut and passed round on little plates with green borders. We were given a fork to eat it with and our glasses were filled with port. Nobody but the Reverend Murray used his fork; we ate the cheese as dalesmen eat it, crushed between finger and thumb. Rabbit jangled down the steps with the last of the crockery and we rose and pushed the two tables together. A lead tobacco jar and box of cigars were placed across the joint. Ted had a bigger pipe than anybody and stuffed it full. I crackled my cigar against my ear; I was not sure what for, but everybody else had done so.

The Colonel rose and held out his glass. 'Gentlemen! The King.'

We followed him to our feet. 'The King.'

Queen Elizabeth II was in her third decade on the throne. 'Why the King?' I asked Ted.

'Society wor formed when William IV wor King – so it's allus the King.'

We sat down again and chairs were pushed back, as the Colonel started his annual report. Rabbit hovered with his tray. Ted turned to me and whispered out of the corner of his mouth, 'This is the bloody crunch – we at the bottom table, becos' we don't pay much, have to buy them buggers up there drink all night.'

Rabbit's fingers stabbed at everybody in turn. 'Double brandy, double whisky, double brandy . . .'

It looked like my dinner was going to cost me a lot more than three guineas. The lordship of the manor is owned by the Drainage Society and this gives us all the right to shoot on the common, take fish with rod or net from the beck and levy fines on the owners of straying stock.

The stalwarts of the Society had, along with the Colonel, 'walked the length' the previous week, and listened to his report intently. Rabbit returned with the drinks. I noticed there was one empty glass in the corner of the tray and there was a marked disparity in the size of the drinks.

The Colonel boomed on. 'No poachers have been prosecuted. There have been no fines for impounding, no revenue from netting rights, no licences to extract issued, but there are monies from grazing the common.'

Rabbit toiled up and down the steps with the big tray. His face was getting redder and redder. Ted pocketed his pipe and reached for two cigars. He passed one to me. Rabbit was puffing into the room with his fourth tray of drinks when the Colonel got to weed cutting. He sniffed and stared at Rabbit, who leaned on the sideboard and ran his tongue over his yellow teeth. He found something fascinating on the floor and his big boot picked at it.

'Last year we engaged Mr Stubley, but the results were far from satisfactory.'

Rabbit was half drunk; his bright red face broke open in a stupid grin and his arms, stretched out each side of him, kept slipping on the sideboard top.

'Well! I had me bad back, I did what I could.'

The Colonel was vexed. He knew Rabbit looked on the job as a sinecure but no one else would have it. Rabbit was voted unanimously into the weed-clearing job again. His grin widened, he collected the tin tray and went about the business of getting the drinks in.

'Why don't yer get trebles and save me owd legs?'

Ted was concerned about the mink which were appearing up the beck – is it the Drainage Society's responsibility to control them? The top table went into a huddle. I pushed back my chair and stretched out my legs under the table. The low-ceilinged room was blue with smoke and, although the fire in the tiny grate had burned low, the room was uncomfortably hot. Rabbit stumbled into the room and left the door open. He banged the tray on to the table and, belching loudly, unloaded the glasses. Tucking the tray back under his arm he made unsteadily for the door and thumped down the steps.

Nobody was listening to the Colonel any more. Ted was fast asleep, hands clasped over his waistcoat, and the six farmers who made up the rest of our table were heavy-lidded, their heads nodded; they were half asleep. Finally, the accounts for the year were finished and the Colonel asked if there was any other business. Two of the farmers were now snoring deeply into their chests. The Colonel banged his gavel and closed the meeting.

'Where's Rabbit with the drinks?'

Rabbit had been missing for half an hour. We found him sitting at the bottom of the steps; the big tray was on his knees and half the glasses were empty. I took the tray from him and his head lolled sideways to clunk against the wood panelling. His voice was quiet, hardly audible, more muttering than talking. 'I git bloody fed up o' cuttin' weed.'

When I got back to the long room the meeting was breaking up. Everyone was standing except Ted, who was still fast asleep. I put the glasses on to the table and awakened him. He came round slowly, staring first at me and then at the backs of the members who were making for the door. He reached out and took one of the full glasses. Holding it carefully in front of him, he rose with several puffs and grunts from his chair and leaned heavily on my shoulder. I had to guide him carefully down the steps, for he was a heavy man and there was no handrail.

We negotiated Rabbit with difficulty. Ted reached down and patted the fat red cheek. 'Tha's a drunken owd bugger.'

Rabbit never moved; he was snoring deeply and evenly.

Charlie was waiting in the lounge. He had a handful of neatly folded squares of paper and gave one to Ted and one to me as I opened the outside door and stepped out into the cold night air. Ted stumbled and struck a match to look at the bill. He passed it to me as the match guttered and his fat fingers grovelled in the box.

'How much is it? I haven't me glasses.'

Charlie's writing was bold and clear. 'It's six quid apiece,' I told Ted.

He staggered off up the village green, his hand fumbling to get the bill back into his pocket. 'Hell's bells, the buggers must have necked some stuff.' I thought of Rabbit sat on the steps, out to the world. The buggers had necked some stuff, but they had had a bit of help.

Ted's tractor drew to a halt outside the shop. He left the engine running because, as he puts it, 'She's a pig to start on a cold morning.' I sat crouched over the one-bar electric fire we kept by the counter, my head in my hands. I am not a good drinker; my youth was misspent acquiring the finer principles of engineering at technical college, unlike Ted and Baz who had served a glorious apprenticeship to John Barleycorn.

Ted was as bright as a button. His cheery red face showed no trace of the gluttony of the previous night. He had left the door wide open and he stood over me, his hands thrust deep into his trouser pockets, the ex-army greatcoat open and pushed back to reveal the thick leather belt and frayed waistcoat shiny with grease.

'Tha looks like a poorly hen.'

I felt like a poorly hen, and although Ted is good company I just wished he would go away and shut the door quietly behind him.

'Ev yer 'ad any breakfast?'

All I needed to make me throw up was for Ted to go into that old corny routine about fatty bacon and raw eggs. I nodded a lie – yes, I'd had breakfast.

Ted seemed reluctant to go. He wandered around the shop, picking up piece after piece. 'Good night, wasn't it?'

I nodded my agreement.

'Bloody expensive, though.'

I remained silent. Money loses its importance when one is in deep and abject misery.

'They're fair though, because they allus invite us to a shoot towards the end o' the season.'

I had no idea when the end of the shooting season was, but I was convinced of one thing – I would not live that long.

Chapter 18

The kitchen was beginning to take on character; we had set a hooky rug before the fire and hung bunches of herbs from the beams. The big pine table, with its harlequin set of chairs around it, was the centre of everything – we ate at it, prepared our food on it and in the evenings Vicky strewed her needlework over its knotty planks while I squatted at one corner with the business accounts. The kitchen was always warm, for we had a good stock of old firewood and we used it generously. The chimney drew well and when I opened the dampers on the flues under the boiler or the oven the flames curled away to flicker and dance up the chimney with a low roar.

The first storms of winter had sent us scurrying into the attic to see if the roof was watertight. Baz had done a good job and every drop of rain was turned into the gutters. The pointing on the end gable had been finished and, apart from the makeshift windows, Christmas Eve found us with a sound, weathertight house.

The children hung their pillowcases each side of the wide fireplace, as Vicky poked sticks under the oven to brown the mince pies. I sat at the table plucking the goose I had bought from Long John. My fingers were sore and I continually changed hands, sending odd feathers floating off the table for the cat to chase as I turned the bird from side to side, its heavy beak clattering on the boards. It was almost midnight when Vicky and I settled in front of the fire with a glass of sherry. With the mince pies cooling on the wire trays and the plump goose filling the biggest willow-pattern meat plate we had, we were ready for Christmas.

I fetched down the children's toys from the top of the linen cupboard and we filled the pillowcases, dropping the usual apple and orange in first. The more homely the kitchen became, the more bleak and uninviting the caravan seemed. Every night we lingered in the kitchen until sheer fatigue drove us to the hard bed. As we gathered up the cat and locked the door behind us the last revellers were turning out of The Ship, shouting their goodnights, and from far down the dale the peal of church bells could just be heard.

Normally we had to drag the children out of bed half an hour before schooltime, but the tiny travelling clock on the corner shelf told me it was not yet seven o'clock on this cold Christmas morning when two little pyjama-clad bodies threw themselves on to our bed.

'The key, the key,' they chanted, 'where is the key?' I fished the big key to the house from my trouser pocket and buried myself back in the warm bed. The children raced off to the kitchen, leaving the caravan door wide open.

Vicky sat up and calculated the cooking time for the goose

on her fingers. I got a sharp prod in the ribs. 'You ought to be getting the oven on.'

The kitchen was still warm as I put the bellows to the little cluster of red coals. I fed chips of dry wood into the tiny flames and soon a hearty fire was roaring in the grate. The oven was still warm to the touch as I opened the flue to send the long flames dancing under it. The dogs were waiting for their walk. If I was late taking them for any reason, they would continually walk up to me and then to the door until I took the hint. This morning they had paraded back and forth across the kitchen until I had turned them into the yard in exasperation. They had crawled under the caravan and sulked. I crammed the goose into the roasting tin and, after ladling honey on to its breast, slipped it into the oven. Calling the dogs, I turned my coat up against the steady drizzle and made for Drover's Lane. The village was deserted, only wisps of blue woodsmoke from the chimneys showed it was inhabited at all.

I kicked off my wellingtons and pulled up my chair in front of the fire. The oven door was too hot for my stockinged feet, so I set them finally on the warm hearthstone and, cupping my hands around the glass of whisky and hot water, I watched the steam rise from my wet trousers. Vicky was at the sink preparing the vegetables and the children played happily on the floor. Sticky kisses had confirmed that the presents were more than acceptable. We had spent more than usual on the children, because they had had no holiday and caravan living had its restrictions. If the weather was bad and they could not take Topic out, tempers would get frayed as they contested for the limited playing space. Caravan life was beginning to wear very thin and we all longed for the day when the new windows would be fitted and we could decorate the house and move in.

We basted the goose every half hour; I crushed a spoon and tied it with string on to a wooden handle, so we could poke it down the side of the roasting tin and baste the bird without taking it out of the oven. Every time we opened the oven door the kitchen was filled with the delicious smell of roast goose, cinnamon and baking apples. We had forgotten to buy a Christmas tree so Vicky had cut a branch of holly and set it in the corner in a bucket of sand. The children had dressed it with homemade decorations, and long strings of coloured streamers, made under the watchful eye of Miss Wells, looped from beam to beam.

I fetched a brown jar from the dairy and set it on the hearth to warm, ready to take the fat from the roasting tin. In the north, goose grease is a remedy for sore throats and 'weak chests'. I told Sally how, as a young boy, I had had many a sore throat treated with it – well rubbed in and then wrapped in flannel, to spend many an uncomfortable winter's night.

She wrinkled her nose in distaste. 'I'd rather have the sore throat.'

The goose grease was really for Rabbit. He used it on the skins he was curing, for after they had been treated with alum and dry wood ash they became as hard as boards. The goose grease made them supple again.

All over Christmas the brown jar stood on the dresser, Sally eyeing it warily occasionally. There was not enough room for all the pans on the bottle-gas cooker, so the potatoes we boiled in a kale pot hanging from a reckon. As we had no lid for the pot and the smoke curled over it from time to time, I whittled a piece of wood clean and dropped it in among the

188

potatoes – any boy scout will tell you this stops them tasting of smoke.

Vicky shuffled the saucepans to and fro and laid the table. Our dinner service was still in store, so no two of the five plates were alike. We had invited Baz and sharp on the stroke of twelve his rain-soaked figure passed the window. I spread his wet raincoat over the fireguard and sat him in a chair with a bottle of brown ale. Baz never touched spirits. 'You can get used to that stuff,' he would say when offered any. As he drank a fair quantity of beer every night, one assumed he wasn't 'used to' that.

Baz pulled two grubby envelopes from his pocket and handed one to each child. There were squeals of delight as they tore them open and pulled out the five pound notes. Peter climbed on my knee and whispered loudly, 'Shall we do it now?' I knew what he meant and nodded my agreement.

The children ran to the holly branch and untied two small packages. They had been painstakingly wrapped and each had a little tag, 'Happy Christmas Mr Baz.' We had been at a loss to know what to buy Baz; he was not one for personal possessions. With Baz a wristwatch would last a week and a lighter no longer, so we had bought him cigarettes. The children had taped a keyring to each packet as their little gifts. Baz held them up to his ears, teasing Sally that they were earrings. Two keyrings for Baz – I don't think he possesses one key.

Peter had taken on the job of keeping Baz's glass filled and fetched another bottle from the dairy. I brought an oil lamp out of the shop and put it in the middle of the table and Vicky set a Christmas cracker by each plate. I dug two forks into the goose and lifted it on to the blue-and-white meat dish. The skin was golden and crisp; we spooned roast potatoes around it and garnished it with rings of apple.

The vegetables were our own produce and we had had hopes of making our own cider, but the tired trees had produced little fruit, so a bottle of white Bordeaux sat out on the rain-lashed window sill to chill. Baz's aversion to spirits extended to wine so Peter kept the beer coming while I plied the rain-speckled bottle between Vicky's glass and mine. I carved one breast of goose and broke a leg away from the carcass for Baz. Vicky heaped his plate to overflowing and he set to with a will. He had no relatives and lived a spartan life. Nearly every meal he ate came out of the frying pan. Bacon seemed to be his staple diet, for he bought several pounds of it from the village shop every week. Along with the quantity of beer he drank every night it must have provided an adequate diet, for he was as strong as a horse and never had a day's illness.

We broke one of our rules and fed the dogs from the table, throwing them crisp bits of skin. Sally nestled the cat on her lap and sneaked bits of meat from her plate for it to nose and sniff at, before it gently took them from her fingers.

The pudding was late. Vicky fished through the folds of linen and prodded it with a fork; it definitely needed longer. Baz leaned back in his chair and lit a cigarette. I swung my chair around to face the fire and poured myself a whisky.

Baz told the children of his early days in an orphanage and of how they had had only one present at Christmas, either an apple or an orange. The children were appalled. 'That's all you got?'

'That was it,' confirmed Baz, 'either an apple or an orange.'

Sally slipped from her chair and ran to the dresser. She took an apple and an orange from the fruit bowl and thrust them into Baz's hands. 'Well, this Christmas you can have both.'

Baz laughed and ruffled her golden hair with his big hand.

There was a catch in his voice as he thanked her. He was a hard-working decent character, without a trace of malice. I think this was the first time he had ever had a real family Christmas dinner.

The pudding was ready at last and Baz stood with the match ready as I poured the tiny bottle of brandy over it. The blue flames licked and flickered, singeing the sprig of holly. No one was hungry enough to do it justice and, after a token amount each, I sat Vicky in a chair with the last of the wine and washed up, while Baz played with the children.

The rain was lashing down when I took the can off its hook and went to milk the goat. I keep a hurricane lamp in the goat house and, as I fumbled for the matches, Elspeth's warm muzzle searched for the dairy nuts. When I got back to the kitchen Baz and the children were laid on the floor around the electric train, filling the trucks with nuts to test the pulling power of the engine. A glass of brown ale stood in the centre of the track and the cat sat alongside it, watching the little engine struggle round with its load. The dogs lay asleep under the table and Vicky sat staring into the fire, her glass empty and her eyes heavy. She has no head for alcohol – three glasses of white wine and her eyes sparkle and she chatters continually, but she soon tires and sleeps like a baby.

I carved the other breast of the goose and made sandwiches, layering the soft meat with apple sauce. Baz and the children took them eagerly but Vicky, half awake, merely shook her head and snuggled deeper into the chair.

At eight o'clock Baz made off to The Ship. As he threw the now dry raincoat around his shoulders, he nodded towards Vicky. 'Come across tonight and bring our lass, it's all on me.'

Vicky slept for over an hour. Her face was beginning to flush with the heat from the fire so I gently drew the chair away from it and took the wine glass from her hand.

We do not like leaving the children, even for a short time, but Vicky had had a hard day and Baz obviously wanted us to have a drink with him, so we put the big nursery fireguard around the hearth and wired it safely to the hob. After ten minutes of do's and don'ts to the children, we bent our heads against the rain and hurried across to the pub.

It was packed. Baz saw us come through the door and waved from the taproom. Charlie set two double brandies in front of us and nodded towards Baz. 'Paid for.' Baz did not let us buy a drink for the rest of the evening. He had instructed Charlie to keep us supplied with brandy. Vicky was no drinker and toyed with her glass, but mine never stayed empty for long. Why Baz had picked on brandy we did not know; it was probably because it was the most expensive spirit in the row of optics.

The people stood three-deep around the bar; villagers who never crossed the pub threshold for the rest of the year ventured in on Christmas night and New Year's Eve. We had had a long, hard day and with the brandy and the hot smoky air my head began to throb. I looked at Vicky; her eyes were half-closed with the smoke and she looked dog-tired. It was time we made for home.

I stuck my head round the taproom door to thank Baz for the drinks. His big arms worked across the table, shuffling dominoes. Ted, Rabbit and the underkeeper took long pulls at their pints. Baz stopped the shuffling and belched. The pint glasses clattered back on to the table. Baz leaned forward intently. 'You hev never seen such a bloody enormous goose, it wor out here.'

The horny hands were held half a yard apart. I called out 'goodnight' and thanked Baz for the drinks.

He turned and grinned at me. 'Hey! I'm just tellin' 'em about that goose.' He shouted the words slowly and carefully. I waved to him and grinned back. I put my hands on Vicky's shoulders and steered her through the crowd to the door.

The fairy lights shone through the milky polythene of our downstairs windows, a haze of pastel around each well-defined circle of colour. The children were lying on the couch, asleep, and under the table the two spaniels could be heard crunching through the carcass of the goose. I opened the kitchen door and shouted them out. Two liver-and-white dogs tucked their behinds in and sped out into the yard, well clear of my ill-aimed boot.

The remains of the goose were pathetic, there was not one piece bigger than a man's finger. The cat sat on the back of the couch, his white-tipped tail flicking to and fro. I picked him up and carried him to the door. Two pairs of sad eyes stared at me from under the caravan. Vicky and I gathered up the children and put them to bed, unwashed and without their teeth brushed – one night would not harm.

We were all late getting up on Boxing Day morning. It was ten o'clock before I had milked Elspeth and fed the poultry. The dogs had spent the whole night under the caravan and came out, tails wagging and heads down, not sure if the previous night's misdemeanour had been forgiven. I called them to heel and set off across the green.

Charlie stood at the pub door, a cigarette stuck firmly in the middle of his mouth and his broad arms folded under the white cotton apron he wore when he did his cellarwork.

'Ow! Just how big was this bloody goose? The more Baz told the tale the bigger it got.'

I looked down at the dogs. 'Well! It was big enough to feed five of us twice and what was left filled two spaniels.'

Chapter 19

New Year's Eve found both Vicky and me in thoughtful mood. We both believe that there are sad houses and happy houses, and ours we felt was going to be a happy one. How could it be otherwise? All the skills and care that had gone into its building, the countless years it had sheltered hard-working farming families, and now the sad years of neglect brought to an end. Once more it felt the heat of a fire and heard the laughter of children.

The four of us sat on the hooky rug in front of a blazing fire, piercing chestnuts with a hatpin and setting them to roast in a long row on the top rib of the grate. The dogs were hard asleep under the table, but the cat perched himself on the milking stool and watched us intently as we threw the hot chestnuts to each other and blew on our fingers.

As the grandfather clock chimed midnight, we hugged and kissed and wished each other a happy new year.

Every morning the Colonel walks around the village with his labrador. He is very much a loner. He sits at the bar in The

Ship most evenings, cradling his whisky glass and staring into space. Our 'evening, Colonel' always brings a polite reply and occasionally a few words, but it is only with Charlie's wife or the vicar that he ever gets into any sort of a conversation. Tourists he completely ignores. He and Ted both sit on the Parish Council, but they do not see eye to eye. Ted wants changes, the Colonel doesn't.

After a meeting, when the Council gathers around the bar, Ted, red-faced at being thwarted once again in one of his schemes, shakes his glass behind the Colonel's back. 'We could have it tarmacked up to the wash-fold if it wasn't for this awkward sod.'

The Colonel will not be drawn. He empties the impedimenta necessary to every pipe-smoker on to the bar and settles himself on his stool.

Rabbit Joe kills the Colonel's moles, Baz does his repair work and Ted's wife goes down three mornings a week to clean for the 'old memsahib', as the Colonel calls his wife. His wife is entirely different; a homely, warm woman, her parents had been bakers. Working themselves to death building up their business from a handcart to a chain of shops, they had left their daughter a sizeable fortune. She likes nothing better than the mornings Dolly comes to clean for her. At eleven o'clock they leave the Colonel alone in his study with his tea, and barter gossip across the kitchen table.

On the first morning of the new year I called the dogs and set off down Drover's Lane to see to Topic. Ted had been muckspreading in the field next to Nellie May's, and a noisy flock of rooks searched the fresh manure for worms. The Colonel was leaning on the gate, watching them intently. We exchanged the usual 'Good morning', without him turning his head. As I broke the ice on the trough he called out to me.

'I see from a card in your window you wish to buy things.'

'That's right, Colonel. Give the best prices in the north of England.'

He knocked out his pipe and peered thoughtfully into the bowl. 'Come across to the house tomorrow morning, ten o'clock.'

I knew he would be a stickler for punctuality so I waited until the shop clock started to chime ten before I started across the green. I knocked loudly on the door. The huge brass knocker sparkled from Dolly's recent attentions. I had never heard so many locks turned and bolts unbolted on one door in my life.

As the Colonel ushered me down the hall and into the study, it was obvious why. The place was crammed with treasures. He gave a disapproving frown towards the kitchen where the old memsahib and Ted's Dolly were laughing over some incident. Closing the study door, he showed me to a large partners desk in the corner.

'Might want to sell some of these.'

Settling himself in a large wing armchair, he busied himself filling a pipe. There was a motley array of Chinese vases and Sheffield plate, and nestled in among them was an early Meissen tankard and cover with the blue-enamelled crossed-swords mark. It was from the first quarter of the eighteenth century and it was a superb piece. I took out my notebook and pencil and, going painstakingly over each piece, I made a list, marking beside each item the price I was willing to give for it. The Colonel poured his tea and watched me in silence.

The Sheffield plate was good-quality stuff but it was all

bleeding quite a lot, and the Chinese vases were late nineteenth-century and mediocre, commercial but in no way desirable. I left the piece of Meissen until last and then, laying my notebook aside, I picked it up and took it to the window. I heard the Colonel return his cup to its saucer and could sense him leaning forward, his eyes on my back. The tankard was obviously very valuable and I felt it was a plant, put there to test me. I held it for a long time, slowly turning it in my cupped hands. It was such a joy to hold; exquisitely painted garlands of flowers and foliage on a ground of pale ivory; the gold lining and silver gilt mounts were of the very best craftsmanship. It was completely out of my class, I would not even make an educated guess at its value. I carried it back to the desk and set it down carefully.

'Well, I can't afford to buy that – it's beautiful.'

We both looked at it in silence for a few moments; a little smile played about the Colonel's mouth – it had been a plant.

He motioned me to a chair and I tore the sheet off my notebook and gave it to him. He searched in the drawer for his glasses and, setting them firmly on his high-bridged nose, he settled back in his chair. He smiled again, more warmly this time. 'Help yourself to tea.'

The study was warm and comfortable. Mounted heads and framed photographs filled every wall except for where a large Victorian gun cabinet stood between two baize-covered doors. The room smelled of gun oil and leather, of tobacco and whisky; it was the essence of masculinity. I could not help looking at the well-stocked gun cabinet. The Colonel saw my interest. He fetched the key from his desk and brought out a pair of Purdeys that were in mint condition. They had been made for his father in 1926 and he confessed that he had never fired them, preferring to use a Holland and Holland sidelock. He had a Sharps express elephant gun and a German deer rifle with telescopic sights. They were all beautifully kept, and the gun cabinet itself was a lovely piece of furniture in well-figured mahogany, with plate-glass doors and little ammunition drawers set under the baize-lined racks. The Colonel had been a good shot in his day, as the mounted heads which lined the hall and study verified. He also had several good clocks dotted about the house and I mused on the fact that a love of guns always seemed to go hand in hand with a love of clocks. He told me of his early days in India as a young subaltern and the great shoots he had been on. On the desk was a silver-framed photograph of him receiving the Military Cross from George VI. He was a fascinating man to listen to and the time flew by.

I heard the back door slam as Ted's wife left at twelve o'clock and it was approaching one o'clock when the memsahib poked her little head through the study door and said that lunch was ready. The Colonel poured two large whiskies while I packed the vases and plate into a cardboard box. I hurried back across the village green, realizing I had made a new friend.

It was some days before I saw the Colonel again. With a twinkle in his eye he confessed he had had the Meissen valued by one of the large auction houses at a considerable, four-figure sum.

Buying from a private source, especially in one's own locality, is fraught with difficulties. In an auction it is plain and simple: if you are willing to give more for that article than any other person in the room at that time, it is yours. The fact that an article has been in the family for generations is completely immaterial to a dealer, it is its worth and its saleability alone which count.

Quite often we have to be the shatterer of dreams. The cherished silver teapot that is only electroplate, the Rockingham dessert service which is a later nineteenth-century copy, and the dreaded worthless Co-op Society sideboard that has been lovingly polished every Friday since new, are stumbling blocks set in the path of every dealer. Many dealers actually refuse to do house calls because of their time-wasting element.

House clearances are hard work. The household goods have to be sorted and often cleaned before they can be passed on to the secondhand dealers, and there is always at least one vanload of rubbish for the tip.

If the children are off school, they delight in a house clearance. They select a sturdy cardboard box and designate it 'the useful box'. They then busy themselves around the house, going through every drawer and cupboard looking for anything which has no real value but could prove useful around the shop or smallholding – string, polishes, cleaning cloths, nails, bowls for feeding ducks and combs for grooming dogs all find their way into 'the useful box'.

One of the most interesting house clearances we ever did resulted from a visit to the shop of a very respectable middle-aged lady. Her bachelor uncle had died recently and she was the sole benefactress. The old man, a retired solicitor, had lived in a well-appointed flat that formed part of a large country house.

The woman, as is usual in these cases, had taken what she required from the flat and wanted the rest cleared. I explained to her that I could not give a price without seeing the goods, but this did not seem to suit her. She wanted us to clear the flat completely and to send her a cheque to cover what we thought was the value. She had already written out on two cards the address of the flat and the address to which the monies were to be forwarded; she dropped these on the counter with the key to the flat. She seemed very agitated and keen to get out of the shop. It was altogether a queer affair – was it a hoax? Were the goods really hers to dispose of? The woman was adamant the goods were hers and that it was a worthwhile job. In the end, I agreed to the terms on the condition that she gave us a signed note to the effect that we had permission to remove the goods and that they were legally hers.

The following day, armed with the letter and the key, I drove up to the house. A thin, frail woman responded to my knock. She showed no surprise when I told her the reason for my visit, merely glancing at the letter authorizing me to clear the flat and leading me down a marble-floored hallway to a white panelled door. I held out my key, but before I could get it in the lock she produced a key of her own and swung the door open before me. Her voice was clipped and terse.

'There are French windows which open on to the patio, it would be better if you took your van round the back.' She turned quickly and clomped her way down the hall.

The pleasant, well-proportioned room was in a state of chaos – obviously large pieces of furniture had recently been removed and piles of books stood about on the carpetless floor. I opened the French windows and drove the van round to the rear. Back in the room, I started to sort through the piles of books. They were all pornographic. Mostly German, they were on good quality paper with full-page colour photographs of the most explicit scenes. A cupboard had been left in one corner and on opening it I found its shelves filled with shoe boxes, each full to capacity with obscene photographs and postcards. A couple of odd balloon-back chairs made up the rest of the furnishings in the lounge.

The bedroom was a different story. It appeared that nothing had been touched. The walls were lined with prints of nudes in various postures, while over the bed a superb oil painting of a large-buttocked nude and a bearded satyr were in a position that left nothing to the imagination. In a deep gilt frame, it was dated 1874 and signed René Magritte. The bedside lamp caught my attention: a finely wrought bronze column depicting cupids prancing around a tree; the delicate octagonal shade was, as I suspected, a lithophane. I switched the lamp on and turned it slowly, its panels depicting a couple copulating in eight different positions.

To one side of the bed stood a bachelor's chest, not a genuine antique but a good 1920s copy. The top drawer was full of the jumble of everyday things; some were ordinary mundane functional items, but some were fashioned into highly skilful erotic forms. There were packs and packs of playing cards, each card sporting a different nude, nutcrackers fashioned from a pair of female thighs, cigar cutters in the shape of women's breasts and, the choicest item of the lot, an enamelled cigarette case which bore a beautiful study of a reclining nude.

A double wardrobe stood against the wall opposite the window, but this revealed nothing more exciting than good quality tweed suits and a dinner jacket reminiscent of the 1920s. The upper shelf was filled with hats, again of good quality, and in the bottom of the wardrobe nestled rows of shoes, all hand-made and well polished. Our gentleman friend had obviously been quite wealthy.

Apart from the photographs and postcards, every item of

erotica was of the best workmanship and superb quality. I sat on the bed and pondered what to do. I was just thankful the children were not here with their 'useful box'. The furniture, what there was of it, was good saleable stuff and the erotica, although not really to my taste, was obviously quite valuable. I started to load the van, starting with the shoe boxes full of photographs. Carefully wrapping the lithophane lamp in a black crombie overcoat, I set it on the passenger seat. By taking the drawers out of the chest I managed to manhandle it into the vehicle.

A small bedside cabinet I had overlooked revealed three pornographic watches in its little drawer. They were of the type given to French soldiers during the First World War, depicting moustachioed poilus having their way with black-stockinged girls.

By four o'clock I had completely filled the van – only the bed and two wardrobes remained. I sought out the frosty-faced landlady and told her I would return for these later that evening.

I drove home more than a little worried about my load of erotica and, leaving the van in front of the shop, carefully locked it.

Vicky was serving a customer but obviously could not wait to hear how I had fared. I walked through the shop into the kitchen and made myself a cup of coffee.

'Well?' she demanded, bursting into the kitchen. 'Was it any good?'

I teased her a little, rolling my eyes and shaking my head. When I had unfolded my story we discussed the problem of what to do with the collection. Sometimes the big auction houses have specialist sales of quality erotica, so we decided to burn the magazines and photographs and lock the remainder of the stuff in the spare bedroom, until it could be dispatched into a suitable auction.

This left the problem of the two wardrobes and the bed. We decided to borrow the Martins's horse box and enlist the help of Baz.

When Baz and I returned, the dour landlady showed even more displeasure as she eyed Baz up and down. Never the most elegant of men, he had come straight from a walling job to give me a hand and still wore his tattered walling jacket. His old boots were caked with clay and his stained moleskin trousers were tucked into their tops. I took all the clothes from the wardrobe and tipped them on to the bed. We filled two plastic sacks with the shoes and dumped them in the trailer.

When I returned to the bedroom, Baz was busy trying on the jackets. They fitted him perfectly. I told him to take what he wanted because the prices we got from secondhand clothes dealers hardly warranted carting them about, so he selected two good quality hacking jackets and a three-piece tweed suit of plus fours.

Baz held the plus fours in front of him and eyed them with approval. 'I've always fancied a pair of shit stoppers.'

I chided him gently that he looked a real gent, and suggested there was a pair of brogue shoes in the trailer which would suit them very well. The thought of Baz in the taproom of The Ship in an elegant suit of plus fours was something to relish.

We cleared the rooms and checked all the cupboards and shelves before we strapped the mattress on the van roof and packed the remainder of the clothes round the furniture to protect it.

The landlady took the key from me silently and stood on the

step watching us as I took the van out of the drive, with the delighted Baz sorting through the plastic sacks of shoes for the brogues. We unloaded the trailer and sheeted up the furniture under the Dutch barn. Baz would not accept any payment but made off home with the bundle of clothes under his arm, as happy as a sandboy.

The following day, when the children were safely off to school, I unlocked the van and made a neat stack in the corner of the yard of the magazines and photos. The glossier type of magazine always burns badly, so I got a forty-gallon oil drum and, after liberally piercing it with a pick axe, started a good wood fire in it before offering the magazines into the flames.

Busty blonde followed busty blonde into the fire, handfuls of cavorting nymphs were quickly devoured and soon the drum glowed red and a pall of ash rose into the morning sky. It was hot work, and I was eager to get through the enormous pile of literature before anyone interrupted me. I found that dousing the books with diesel before forking them into the flames speeded up the process.

It was two hours before I spiked the last voluptuous nude on my fork and cremated her. It must have taken the old man the best part of his lifetime, and many hundreds of pounds, to acquire such a collection.

I was now faced with the problem of assessing the value of the remaining goods. I sat at my little desk in the shop making a list and marking a reasonable price beside each item. Some of the erotica was of such quality there would be no problem passing it on, but a lot of it, although worthwhile, led into the grey areas of bad taste. I finally arrived at a figure and, deducting a small amount for my morning's labour at the furnace, I sent off the cheque. Remembering the woman's obvious agitation, I decided against including a list of articles and merely sent a covering letter stating that the enclosed cheque was for the goods removed as agreed.

That night the lounge of The Ship was empty, but the tap-room was packed to overflowing. There was laughter and guffaws as postcards were passed from little group to little group.

Charlie looked round momentarily as I went down the steps. 'Be with you in a minute,' he said as he returned his attention to the postcard Ted was holding.

It was of a large-buttocked lady of the type beloved by Rubens. With her milk-white face and prim little mouth, she had the look of the 1920s about her. Ted held the card a foot above his head and turned to Baz who was standing in front of the fire, proudly wearing his new plus fours. 'How much for this one?'

Baz grinned broadly. 'You can have her for a quid.'

The trade was brisk; a pound per postcard seemed to be the going rate. Charlie brought me a pint down to the taproom and I pushed my way across to Baz. He was stuffing pound notes into the waistcoat pocket of his new suit. I was about to compliment him on his new turnout, when he turned to me with a big grin. 'By, yon fella must have been a wicked old bugger. Every pocket of them coats was filled with mucky pictures.'

The Colonel sidled up to us; he was holding three sepia-and-white postcards, each showing a group of thin oriental-looking girls posed among ferns and potted plants.

Baz eyed them authoritatively. 'Ah, them's what's known as collectables, Colonel – a fiver the three.'

The blue note disappeared into the waistcoat pocket. More and more postcards were bought from Baz and note after note found its way into his waistcoat pocket. I must have burned a king's ransom.

I suddenly remembered that there were still several suits in a heap in the apple house, probably harbouring more photographic delights. When Baz had completely sold out of postcards, I took him aside and suggested that there might be more in the remaining suits. He was delighted at the idea. He placed his half-empty glass on the mantelpiece and was making off on his quest when I pulled him back by the arm. 'We'll go halves on this lot.'

He nodded his agreement and within ten minutes he was back with a thick wodge of postcards. 'Fresh supplies, lads,' he announced, standing at the top of the taproom steps.

Again the little groups formed and laughed and joked as the cards were passed round.

Baz found two more cards of the sad little oriental girls and pressed them on the Colonel. 'There must have been a set of five,' he told him. 'We don't want to break up a set, do we?' The Colonel responded with three one-pound notes. Baz was revelling in his new-found wealth and the pints flowed freely.

The old day had barely half an hour of it left as I made my way unsteadily across the village green and upstairs to bed.

The morning after found me very much the worse for wear. I had risen late and Vicky had already fed the stock and milked the goat. I sat at the pine table, my head in my hands.

Vicky thumped a mug of black coffee in front of me; I winced at the noise. 'Porno merchant,' she said scathingly, as she slammed the kitchen door behind her.

Chapter 20

I looked out of the window at the grey sky. The first small flakes of snow fell, gently powdering the road and wash-fold track; they tinted the grass on the village green, turning it a pale sage. I had a house call to make up the dale and I did not like the look of the weather. The worst of the winter snows start like this – big soft flakes, and the snow is gone by mid-afternoon, but these small ones, hard and frozen, have more staying power. It only needs the west wind to get up and start whipping it into flurries to make a dales farmer bring down his sheep from the fell and check the log pile.

I threw the snow chains into the back of the van and flagged down Ted's grey Ferguson. 'What's the best way to Harts Ghyll?'

'Through Middlethwaite, turn left at t'Brown Cow and keep straight on past t'King's Head. Is it Mrs Price's you're off to?' I told him it was. 'Pop thi head into her parlour; she has the finest graithing of pewter on her dresser tha'll ever see.' He grated the Fergie into gear and thrust his head through the canvas hood again. 'Watch thissen' up there, this weather.'

The road narrowed down to a single white strip and the van wheels were just beginning to slip as I made the crest of the hill. The old woman was keeping a lookout for me and she waved from the window. It was a particularly nice oak press she had to sell, an honest country piece of good colour.

Covering the kitchen table was a motley collection of salt-glazed pancheons and a glistening white bedpan.

'Never been used,' she assured me.

They are terrible things and completely unsaleable. I have a pile of them behind the Dutch barn, carefully stacked so they don't crack with the frost. Ted had shaken his head in disbelief when I had brought them to his attention. 'No home should be without one.'

The old woman accepted the price I offered, so I loaded the van and then counted out the notes on to the kitchen table. She was visibly agitated and, when I held out the bundle of notes and asked her to check it for me, she stuffed it into her pinafore pocket. 'It'll be all right.'

She had the kettle boiling on the hob and when we pulled up to the fire with our cups of tea she told me the cause of her concern. She had never had so much money in her hand in her life. 'Where can I put it? I'll never sleep tonight.'

I bundled her into the van and drove her down to the Post Office in Middlethwaite. The travelling butcher's van was parked outside The Brown Cow, so while Mrs Price was opening a Post Office savings account I walked across the slippery cobbles and took two pork and apple pies from the zinc shelf. Thievin' Jack's pies have a reputation second to none.

I hadn't closed the van door behind me before the pub window opened and Thievin's pink hand thrust out towards me.

'I thought I'd got away with a couple, Jack,' I joked as I dropped my money into it.

'No chance, son. I can hear the creak of that there van door half a mile away.'

The snow was now coming down thickly, but with the weight of the press in the back the van made it back up the hill to Mrs Price's with no difficulty.

Fresh tyre tracks scythed off the road up past the wash-fold into the yard. Fiery's van stood by the barn, two pairs of footprints leading from it into the house. Little Petal sat at the table, a woollen shawl pulled around her ample shoulders and the biscuit jar at her elbow. Vicky had given her a pile of women's magazines to look at and she flicked through their pages aimlessly.

Fiery slid out of my chair and squatted on a milking stool. 'Owt in my line, guv?'

I told him of the pancheons and the bedpan. He wrinkled his nose. 'Bedpans, unsaleable goods, guv.'

Little Petal looked up from her magazine. 'Fiery, tell them about *your* unsaleable goods.' She licked a grubby thumb and flicked over several pages until she came to a picture of a huge chocolate cake. 'Up in front of the beak, Wednesday morning he was.'

Fiery hugged his knees and grinned up at me. 'Got done for unlawful possession of a firearm. Did a house clearance near Rochdale; there was this big wardrobe stuffed with old bedding and when I sorted it through I found a pillowcase that had £140 in it an' this Luger pistol.' Fiery rocked back on the stool. 'Couldn't resist it, guv. I took it into the quarry and had a go wi' it.' He raised his right hand and squinted down two fingers. 'Per-ching, per-ching – it wor real. Anyhow, this old sod saw me and bubbled me.' His voice went quiet. 'Boys in blue wor knocking at the door when I got back.'

He stretched his short legs and thrust his hands between his thighs. Little Petal's dirty fingernail scored a line under the answer to 'Worried Blueyes'. 'An' tell him how much you got done.'

Fiery's bright eyes looked up at me, a shy grin on his face. 'A hundred and forty quid.'

Snowballs thudded on to the windowpanes. The children had been let out of school early. They stamped into the kitchen, pink-faced and out of breath. 'Where's our sledges?' they demanded.

The sledges were stuffed into the rafters of the apple house along with Cedric, a well-mounted crocodile we had acquired at auction. No bids had been forthcoming for the six-foot-long monster, so the auctioneer had combined it with the next lot, a Regency writing table. I'd got them for a reasonable price and, although the table went quickly, Cedric proved unsaleable. I had put him in the shop as an interest piece with a modest price tag hanging from his fearsome teeth, but there had been no takers. Small children were either frightened of him or threw screwed-up sweet wrappers deep into his pink throat. Cedric's knobbly skin was a great gatherer of dust and he took up valuable floor space in the small shop, so he had been relegated to the apple house.

Fiery bumbled around the furniture, asking the price of everything. He selected a set of cart-horse gears, several oak-framed prints and a poor jug-and-bowl set. We carried them carefully down the snow-covered steps and put them in his van, along with the pancheons. We slammed the van door shut and stood and looked up at the snow-filled sky.

'You'll not get over the tops tonight, Fiery.'

He thrust his hands deep into his pockets and looked up at me thoughtfully. 'Do you think Charlie'll put us up at The Ship?'

Charlie was delighted to accommodate the couple, so Little Petal waddled through the snow to the village shop to buy toothbrushes and the odd little things a girl needs for a night away from home. Fiery joined the children sledging down the garth.

It was a happy group that jostled up to the table as Vicky brought the big brown stewpot from the oven. Little Petal had bought six packets of biscuits and she shyly placed a pile by each plate. After the meal was over, the children claimed her. She squatted in the corner with them, taught them how to do the cat's cradle, recited nursery rhymes they had never heard and sang funny little songs until her head drooped on to her chest.

Fiery gently put the wool shawl around her shoulders. 'Come on, Pet, let's get you to bed.'

Although the concern he showed for her was genuine, he had an ulterior motive in seeing her off to bed at eight o'clock: he wanted a night in the taproom with the boys.

It is not easy to leave a warm kitchen for a chilly caravan. Every night we lingered by the fire as long as we could before going through our little end of the day ritual of banking up the fire, filling the side boiler and gathering up the cat.

I left Vicky fishing the reluctant animal from under the table and wandered into the lounge to peer through the windows to assess conditions outside. I was surprised to see a little group of people gathered below the wash-fold. The tall figure in a mackintosh and bobble hat was unmistakably Rabbit. He was continually flashing a torch towards the wash-fold. Fiery Frank and Charlie stood in conversation. Both had a bottle of beer, and the little man used his to point to where Rabbit's torch flashed. I called Vicky into the lounge and we watched the little group for a few minutes, before curiosity got the better of us. We grabbed our coats and went out on to the village green.

Ted took me by the arm. 'It's just eaten one of Rabbit's best terriers.'

Rabbit shone the torch into the wash-fold for my benefit: there stood Cedric dripping wet and in front of him the scuffled snow was red with blood. Curtains were being pulled back all round the village green. Two or three more villagers had joined the little group, before the flashing blue light of a police car announced the arrival of Sergeant Tate. Never a man to lose his dignity, he strode unhurriedly through the crowd. Before he could get out the time-honoured, 'What's going on here?', Ted and Rabbit collared him.

'A bloody crocodile! Just eaten one of Rabbit's terriers.' Rabbit flashed his torch again, reflecting the malevolent eyes, the dripping jaws and the awesome, blood-stained snow.

The good sergeant reacted quickly. Here at last was a situation which, handled correctly, could put the coveted chrome pips of an inspector on his shoulders. He delegated Ted, Rabbit and myself to keep back the crowd and ran off to the Colonel's house.

The Colonel was just finishing what had been a very good bottle of port and was none too pleased to be interrupted by some idiot babbling on about a crocodile on the village green. He took the .22 rifle from the gun case and a pack of ammunition and handed them to the elated sergeant.

Shouting excitedly to the crowd to keep back, the sergeant broke open the pack of bullets and, slipping one into the breech, flattened himself in the snow, calling for Rabbit to keep his torch on the crocodile. A second or two to steady his aim, then a clear sharp crack rang out across the village green.

Cedric never flinched; a second shot followed before the sergeant got to his feet and advanced in a crouched manner towards his adversary. He thrust the muzzle of the gun into Cedric's mouth and flipped him over on his back.

The little crowd cheered and clapped. Sergeant Tate drew himself up to his full height and uttered a very unpoliceman-like expletive. He walked slowly back to the crowd, which by now was completely silent. Neither Ted nor Rabbit was anywhere to be seen.

'All right,' he said, taking out his notebook, 'who is the bloody joker?'

Nobody said a word. He went from person to person in exasperation, to be met by sniggers and guffaws. The little crowd melted away, leaving the furious sergeant trying to stuff the six-foot crocodile into the panda car. The only way he could get it in was by winding down both rear windows and letting Cedric's snout stick through one window and his tail through the other.

The Colonel rodded the rifle and wiped it carefully with an oily cloth, then emptied the box of cartridges on to the study desk and counted them carefully. He eyed the sergeant coldly. 'New box, twenty-five cartridges, two shots fired, twenty-two cartridges on the desk, one missing.'

As Vicky and I locked the kitchen door and made for the caravan, the hapless policeman's torch could be seen criss-crossing the trampled snow looking for the missing bullet.

*

213

The following night the taproom of The Ship was full. Ted and Rabbit had never had so much beer bought for them in their lives. Every detail was gone through lovingly – how the crocodile had been dragged through the snow to make convincing tracks, doused with water and red ink splashed about the scuffed snow in front of it. It was well past closing time when the towel was placed on the pumps. Ted drained his glass and banged it on to the mantelpiece. 'Yon little feller in t'red weskit is a comic.'

He laughed and made his way unsteadily up the steps to the lounge. Rabbit was laid full length on the floor. One of the underkeepers from the Estate volunteered to take him home, but his big frame proved too much for one man.

As we got him into his cottage and dropped him into a chair, he opened one bleary eye and smiled up at us. 'Eh! I wonder if I can claim for me terrier?'

We were not worried about the loss of the unsaleable Cedric. He stands to this day in the enquiry room of Lalbeck police station, two neat little holes between his eyes and a collecting tin for the Police Benevolent Fund hanging from his glistening teeth.

Chapter 21

It was the second week in January, a grey drizzly afternoon. I saw the Colonel crossing the village green with his labrador at his heel. He walked up to the house and I heard the letterbox clatter. It was a cryptic note, written with an ink pen in a bold hand.

'Invitation to shoot Wednesday 09.00 hours meet my house.'

That night in The Ship I sought out Rabbit Joe to ask his advice. Rabbit always acted as one of the beaters on these occasions and would know the form. I had done a little shooting before but had never been on an organized shoot, with driven pheasants. I confessed to Rabbit that I had no proper shooting clothes and that my only gun was a rather antiquated double-barrelled Greener. According to Rabbit, there would be no problems. Every year Ted apparently brought an old hammer gun he had inherited from his grandfather; the only problem, said Rabbit, was in staying well clear of the Colonel, who blasted away in a 120-degree arc at everything that moved.

On Wednesday morning I was on parade at the Colonel's five minutes before the appointed time. The evening before, I had spent a good hour and a half discussing with Vicky what to wear and had finally decided upon corduroys, hiking boots and waxed jacket, topped off with a deerstalker-type hat. It was the best I could manage.

My fears about its aptness vanished completely when Ted appeared up the Colonel's drive. It looked as though he had not only acquired the gun from his grandfather but his suit also. It was a rough-spun tweed of almost pinkish hue, the plus fours and long waistcoat spoke of an earlier age, the jacket was patched and its pockets bulged with cartridges and sandwiches. He had a red spotted handkerchief at his neck and on his head sat the largest checked cap in captivity.

Rabbit put his hand on Ted's shoulder and turned to me, a broad grin on his face. 'There's a notice in his shop window – "Antiques bought", tha wants to take this suit over, Ted, and see what he'll give thee for it.'

Ted was not amused. He was proud of his 'gentleman's suit'. With the exception of the occasional funeral it saw the light of day only twice a year, at the Drainage Society dinner and the annual shoot.

The Colonel appeared at nine o'clock prompt and led us down Drover's Lane and across the twenty-five-acre to the Estate office. We nodded our greetings to the rest of the Drainage Society. Looking round, I saw that Ted's outfit now appeared quite normal and modest. I had never seen such a motley gathering of old clothes – it was like a mobile Oxfam shop. Cardboard boxes of cartridges were brought out and broken open. The Estate servants came round with a tray of whisky; the generous helpings of smooth malt felt warm and

216

comforting on the cold January morning. The Colonel and Mr Fairbrother had a long and quiet discussion about the placing of the guns. It was normal to draw lots in sequence right to left, facing the beaters, but on an occasion like this so many of us were not regular shooting men and had not a trained dog with us. My two springers, although coming from the best stock in the land, had never been trained to the gun.

It was decided that one dog would have to work with two or even three guns, so the men with the best dogs were called out and the rest of us drew lots from a keeper's hat. I was the second to draw and drew number one, which put me on the extreme right. Ted went next and drew a ticket with an elaborate movement of the arm.

'Six and seven eighths,' he announced, with a beaming smile. Apparently it was his annual joke. I was quite relieved to find he had drawn number two and so would be on my left-hand side.

I filled my pockets with cartridges and moved off into position. The beaters had been taken off earlier and we could hear their whoops and shouts and sticks thrashing the bushes. I felt a little apprehensive because I was right on the Estate boundary, no more than twenty yards from the road to Bedale. I had a vague recollection that it was illegal to shoot less than fifty yards from a main road, but no one seemed to care about these things.

We walked line abreast across the first field without a bird rising in front of us, when I noticed that on my left it was not Ted but the Colonel.

'Bloody dog, bloody dog,' he was shouting, as the labrador bounded in front of him. He saw my head turn his way and called out, 'A man with a dog between two of them that haven't.'

I remembered Rabbit Joe's warning and shuddered. To my far left the reports of guns rang out, indicating that the line had reached rising pheasants, but nothing came on our side. The shoot was to be a shared bag affair and I felt rather glad of it.

Ted had swung at a rising cock pheasant and missed; nothing at all had risen in front of the Colonel or me. We scaled a rickety slab-wood fence and crossed marshy ground to stand fifty yards in front of a well-grown covert. I could hear the beaters crashing their way through the brush, but all the birds slipped away to our left.

The Colonel's labrador made off, hell bent for the covert. The Colonel, red in the face, shouted after it, 'Bloody dog, bloody dog.'

We stood in line until the covert was beaten out. One bird rose before me. It flew directly above me so I swung my gun high above my head, fired and missed. Its speed was deceptive and I should have followed through. The old adage, 'aim a rifle and point a shotgun', came back to me. Another bird broke near to my left. I swung in a good arc at shoulder height, squeezed the trigger and saw it tumble in a flurry of feathers into the grass.

I had not heard the Colonel fire at all, but he marched forward with confident stride. 'My bird, I think,' he said, scooping it into his game bag.

We worked down the contour of the land in a long line, skirting the forty-acre town pasture now ploughed and set with winter wheat. As we stood in a huddled group on the bank of the beck, hip flasks were produced and Ted waddled up to me to proffer a corned beef sandwich, a good cock pheasant swinging proudly from his belt. I told of my little *contretemps* with the

218

Colonel and how he had claimed what had obviously been my bird.

'Oh, he will, he will,' replied Ted. 'He can't see, ya know – don't get in front of him, whatever tha does.'

A rough bridge of railway sleepers crossed the beck. I squatted on it, peering into the crystal clear water. In summer it was a fruitful beck full of bullheads, caddis fly larvae and sleek brown trout. On this clear, cold morning nothing could be seen in the bright water as it rushed among the bent reeds. The beaters had been taken off to work the bottom plantation; pheasants had been fed here all winter and, although it had been heavily shot over in the autumn, it was expected that there would be a good draw.

The gamekeeper blew on his whistle and we fanned out across the field, keeping to our original stations. I watched the Colonel nervously – having received two warnings I was definitely not going to get in front of him. Once again, we could hear the sticks and cries of the beaters. At the end of the season the pheasants that are left tend to be more wary and break cover later. The beaters were almost on the edge of the wood before the birds broke cover; they came thick and fast, some swooping low to the ground and others skying in a desperate attempt to get over the guns. I let fly with a left and a right and missed both my birds – my reaction was too slow.

The Colonel blasted away with surprising rapidity. He was clearly elated, lead shot hissed over my head. He got three shots off to my every one, but with the same results. I pulled up the collar of my coat and crammed the deerstalker hard on to my head, tying the earflaps under my chin.

Ted's suit and cap afforded him less protection. 'It's like Hell Fire Corner,' he complained.

The majority of birds had broken down the valley well to the left, which was as anticipated, and many had fallen to the better shots. The beaters came out of the wood to join us and we made our way down the valley to a small derelict barn, where the Estate wagon had drawn up. Two trestle tables were laid with immaculate white cloths and set out with game pie, pâtés and cheeses. Dolly dished out hot jacket potatoes. Paper cups were handed out and the underkeeper came round and filled them with a good Beaujolais. The Colonel and Mr Fairbrother stood at the tailgate of the Land-Rover, a bottle of brandy set before them. The Colonel's labrador had returned and lay panting under the vehicle.

'Lost me bloody dog,' he said to Ted.

Mr Fairbrother wandered off to have a word with the beaters. Ted gave me a broad wink and went up to the Colonel.

'The dog's down there with Charlie Bowls.' The Colonel grunted and made off to find his dog. Ted drew out his hip flask and filled it to the brim from the brandy bottle. 'The buggers had enough out of us at the Drainage dinner,' he said, filling my paper cup with brandy.

After lunch we worked our way back up Fox Covert and raised very few birds. Elated with drink, I happily blasted away at birds, all hopeless shots.

As we made our way back to the barn, Rabbit Joe appeared out of the covert. 'How have you done?'

I held up my hand in a helpless gesture. With a grin, he produced two fine cock birds from under his coat. I tied them to my belt.

It was four o'clock before we made our way back to the barn and threw our birds into a long line. As the underkeepers came round with more cups of whisky the head keeper counted the bag, prodding each bird as he did so with his long stick. The bag was shared out and I made my way home with three good fat pheasants, two cocks and a hen.

The generous whiskies and brandies had had more than a slight effect on me and, as I passed through the shop on my way to the kitchen, I took an elaborate masonic medal from a showcase and hung it round my neck. I plucked and dressed the pheasants, for we never like hanging them. Peter was sent round to Nellie May's with the hen. As we sat down to dine off pheasant, turnip and potatoes, with a good white sauce and a bottle of burgundy, the medal still jangled at my neck.

'What's that for, Daddy?' Sally enquired.

'That, my dear, is for showing calmness and dedication to duty at Hell Fire Corner.'

There is a long tradition of poaching in the village; situated as it is between a large sporting estate and the moors, the opportunities have always been there, and there have always been men ready to take up the opportunities.

Poaching is largely for the family table. Commercial poaching is confined to the netting of grouse a day or two before the season opens, when a hundred or so brace will be consigned to London to appear on the dinner tables of the top-class hotels on the glorious twelfth. 'Shot on the Yorkshire Moors this morning', will be the proud boast. I often wonder if the well-heeled diners ever ponder the fact that there is no shot in the birds.

The poaching of pheasants is a less organized affair but hardly anyone in the village goes through the shooting season without having had an Estate pheasant on the plate before them, and whether it comes there legally or not nobody really cares.

The long stone wall, a good eight feet high, which forms the northern boundary of the Estate, had been built to give work to the locals during depressed times. Its flat-dressed stone coping is a favourite perching place of pheasants during snow or a heavy frost. The plump birds strutting along the wall in the wintry sunshine tempt many a man. When anyone in the village is offered a brace the usual query is, 'Have they come off the wall?'

The Reverend Sidney Murray carries more weight than is good for him. With three parishes to care for he is a busy man, but he never neglects the pleasures of the table. His wife Stephanie is the epitome of the country parson's wife; she runs the church groups and the Reverend Sidney with an iron hand. Viewing the good churchman's increasing waistline with concern, and forever wrestling to keep up appearances on a small stipend, she hit upon the ideal solution – she would buy the Reverend Sidney a bicycle. It would reduce his waistline and the petrol bills at the same time.

Sidney hates it; he lets down its tyres, feigning punctures, and often employs a little gentle sabotage to enable him to keep the detested machine in the shed and get out his beloved Morris Minor. Stephanie is no fool and was soon on to his little ploys. The church warden is one of those fortunate men who have an affinity with all things mechanical; under his capable hands the most recalcitrant of engines bursts into life, nuts never become cross-threaded and bearings run like silk. Stephanie soon put the care of the bicycle into his capable hands and, no matter what abuse the good vicar subjects it to, an hour or two with the church warden soon returns it to roadworthiness. Only the filthiest of weather makes Stephanie relent and let Sidney use the little Morris Minor.

It was a fine, cold January morning, an iron frost gripped the still countryside under a steel-blue sky, as the Reverend Sidney bicycled alongside the long wall. He had seen numerous pheasants squatting or strutting silently along its mile length, but as he breasted the little rise below Folly Hill a particularly fine specimen caught his eye. It was a plump young ring-necked cock, full-breasted and with a sheen on its feathers which caught the wintery light.

The Reverend watched the pheasant strut and preen itself for a good two minutes. Men of the cloth are subject to the same temptations as lesser mortals, and it was not long before the good gentleman laid his bicycle on the grass verge and selected a sizeable piece from a branch of dead elm. His aim was accurate and unerring and the bird fell dead at the other side of the wall.

The problem now was how to retrieve it. He leaned his bike against the wall and, standing on the saddle, he could see the bird lying below him in the frosted grass, its neck obviously broken. The problem was not how to get over the wall, but how to get back with his spoils. He was on the point of abandoning his prize when he remembered a summer's afternoon he and Stephanie had spent following the beck from Folly Hill in search of whirled water milfoil along its marshy banks. The beck had passed through the long wall under a small stone arch, not more than thirty yards from where he now stood. He tested the frozen beck with two or three good stamps and was soon on all fours and through the arch. Scooping up the choice pheasant he stuffed it under his coat and regained the arch. The return passage was not easy. The beck had frozen in a series of tiny cataracts and Sidney puffed and wheezed as he wriggled into the arch.

He was nearly through when he received two sharp and painful kicks in his left buttock. The underkeeper had watched the little charade from behind an oak. He had meant to let the Reverend have his bird, but the sight of the ample rump, tight in clerical grey, had proved too much.

The Reverend hobbled home, the pheasant swinging from his crossbar, his mind working furiously on a suitable explanation for his injury. He surveyed the bruised buttock in the cheval mirror and winced. Why were underkeepers always such brutal types, with big feet? To explain his limp he told Stephanie he was having his old cartilage trouble again, and he lowered himself carefully into the study chair for her to massage the innocent knee.

The tale was soon round the village, but nobody thought any the worse of Reverend Sidney for his little escapade. It was a week or two before he showed himself in The Ship again. Everyone was careful to avoid talk of pheasants, except Ted. With a twinkle in his eye he subjected the vicar to a lecture on pheasants, listing every natural enemy they had and every disease and ailment they were subject to.

Finally, draining his glass he thumped it on the counter. 'Aye,' he said, turning from the bar, 'they can be a right pain in the arse, can pheasants.'

Chapter 22

After Christmas we were tempted to put a bed in the kitchen and sleep in there rather than the caravan, but this would have been unfair on the children. The little stove in the caravan was never lit any more; instead we propped up a fan heater on a pile of books and let it hum away for an hour before the children went to bed.

It was the last week in January when the new windows arrived. I painted around the edge of each one with red lead paint, before I let the joiner fit them. They were so expensive I felt that they would have to last my life out, at least. My hotch-potch of picture glass and polythene, which had effectively kept out the winter storms, was stripped from each window and cast into the yard. The new frames were fitted and glazed in two days. Robin stepped back on to the green and surveyed his work.

'You'll have to get a lick of paint on them as soon as you can – the birds'll go for the new putty.'

I knew what he meant the following morning, as I climbed

the ladder, paintbrush in hand, for already the tits' beaks had stippled little marks into the lower fillets of putty. They like the linseed oil it contains.

We have insulated the loft to a high level and, with a heavy curtain behind the front door, the house is quite warm. The feeble radiators in the hall and on the landing take the chill out of the air, but the landing remains a place to hurry across, barefoot, on the way to the bathroom.

The kitchen is still the heart of the house; always warm and comfortable, it is our cocoon. The walls are cluttered with objects. We are great hangers-up of objects. There is a spoon rack, a salt box, a case containing a pair of kingfishers, two shotguns, a pipe rack, a pair of martingales, a glass rolling pin and at least a dozen prints. The children have the short wall to the right of the range, and this is festooned with bold paintings in primary colours, interesting leaves and fruits and all the things children wisely recognize as precious and worth keeping. Two or three horsebrasses wink through the mass of herbs and drying onions which clutter around the oak beams. It is not a sparkling clean, antiseptic kitchen by any means and, as Vicky battles to keep its happy jumble acceptably clean, she consoles herself that it is always better than Dolly's. Dolly's is a muck 'ole, a warm, friendly, seedy, comfortable, cow-smelling muck 'ole and I like it, but it is a muck 'ole.

Only the kitchen had felt the paintbrush, the stripped pine doors had been waxed once and the wax had sunk in so they looked as though they had never been touched. The plaster had dried out a pale grey, the colour of a wood-pigeon's breast, and we had hung several large coaching prints in the hallway and up the stairs. A variety of rugs had been scattered throughout the house – old hand-worked rugs and squares of carpet we had picked up at the sales and from house clearances, and washed in the beck.

The house was warm and comfortable so we decided to live in it and leave all the decorating until the spring. A lick or two of paint and a square yard or two of wallpaper was all that is required – mere frippery.

Ted towed the caravan into the garth for us but we hadn't the heart to put the torch to it, as we had long vowed we would do. The ducks took to living under it, so we ripped out the fittings and used it for storage.

Baz had been a tower of strength; daunting tasks fell before him like grass before a scythe. The cigarette would be trodden out and he would set to with a will. 'Come on, let's get it bossed.' We wanted to buy him something to mark the completion of the house, but he was impossible to buy for. The things he needed were legion, but he wanted for nothing.

'Let's give him a party,' suggested Sally, and so the idea of a party for Baz grew into a housewarming party. We would invite everyone who had helped us.

Thievin' Jack the butcher always finished his round early on Thursdays. The converted Bedford wagon, with its high aluminium body and its Perkins diesel, groaned and rocked its way past the wash-fold and on to the top of the village green, the drooping iron step barely clearing the lumps in the track.

Mrs Lewis eased her pinafored body down the counter and moved the packets of washing powder to one side of the small window ledge, so she could keep an eye on Jack. They have an agreement: she does not sell sausages and he does not sell eggs. She does not trust Jack and neither does anyone else. Vicky always makes sure she has a five-pound note ready for him because whatever the value of the note tendered he always gives change for a fiver. Dolly was philosophical about it.

'At least he smiles when he robs you; the bugger we had before robbed you and scowled.'

Thievin' bowed to the carriage trade – the van stopped outside the Colonel's gate and Mrs Smythe-Robinson's – but the rest of the villagers had to toil to the top of the green for their meat.

Thursday was a good day for Thievin' Jack. The farmers gathered in The Ship after the mart had money in their pockets and, although it is not an easy task tempting money from a farmer's pocket, Thievin' Jack had a good ally in John Barleycorn. The little scrubbed zinc counter was covered with several good joints – lean grainy hunks of flesh half husked with a thin layer of marbled fat awaited men who knew what they were looking for.

His meat was good; he hung it longer than the town butchers. His pies and sausages were unbeatable. Fat, bloated sausages with mottled skins that wept clear golden fat into the hot pan. Thievin' was a glib salesman; he would slap the meat on to the tiny counter, his pink hands throttling it as he smiled and lifted the lean end for his customer's appraisal.

'No old milk beast this, luv – best bull beef.' A broad wink and the smile grew ear to ear. 'Put some lead in your Charlie's pencil, eh!' The joint was swept on to the scale, Thievin' leaned close to his customer. 'To you, luv, six quid.' There were mild protests at the price. Thievin' leaned back and steeled his knife. The easy smile came again. 'Best meat in England, and I'm damn near givin' it away.'

There have been rebellious husbands who drove their wives into Lalbeck for two or three Saturday mornings in search of cheaper meat, but they all ended up back in Thievin' Jack's little van.

I had measured the meat tin carefully. I wanted to get the biggest joint of beef we could cook. Thievin' looked up from his cutting board and grinned. 'One foot ten by what?' I turned the scrap of paper with the measurements towards him. He wiped his hands on his apron and picked it up. 'That's a big piece of beef, owd lad. Gawd, that'll weigh summat – mother-in-law coming up for t'weekend, is she?'

I told him it was for the housewarming we were having. He turned and opened the shelved cupboard at the back of the van. His fingers tapped on the zinc door. 'What about this and this?'

Two big lean joints were drawn out of the cupboard. 'No,' I told him, 'it must be one joint that size – for effect.'

'Oh, for effect.' The fingers tapped again and he started to whistle.

A huge haunch was drawn out and dossed on the counter, he thrust his hands deep into the pockets of the white bloodstained smock. 'That'll be too big, but I can cut it.'

I measured it with a cloth tape. It was two inches too short.

'It's the biggest I've got,' Thievin' said, a little hurt.

It was too big for the scales so he hung it on a spring balance from the van roof; the needle hovered at nineteen pounds.

'How much?'

'Well, it's best bull beef, I could do it for –' there was a long pause – 'forty-eight quid.'

We were both staring at the joint, Thievin' with his hands on his hips. A drop of blood splattered on the van floor.

'It's a bit dear, Thie . . . er, Jack.' We stared at the joint in silence.

'What kind of do are yer having, just family, like?'

I told him that Ted and Dolly, Baz, Rabbit and all the tap-room lot were coming.

Jack grinned. 'Tha will want a big piece then, 'cos they're wide-necked buggers.'

There was more silent staring, followed by another splat of blood.

'Half the village coming, eh?' I told him it was so. 'Well, now –'

I knew what he was after. 'We'd like you and Ivy to come.'

Jack's grin was ear to ear. 'Tell thee what, tha can 'ave it for forty-five quid.'

With the meat wrapped in muslin and hung from the dairy roof, and one of Mrs Lewis's best cheeses nestling on the highest stone shelf, it just left the drinks to be organized. Beer for the men, punch for the women. The beer was easy: Charlie, wise in the ways of the 'wet' trade, ordered us three pins from the brewery – thirteen and a half gallons. I stabbed at the calculator in the shop – over a hundred pints, should do. The redoubtable Mrs Beeton gave us a recipe for the punch and Vicky nipped along to the shop in search of nutmeg and other spices.

The impending party was good for trade. The villagers popped into the shop for a tin of wax or a plate-stand; now the word had got round that we were inviting almost everybody. Vicky and I used the same technique. 'Will you pop across and have a drink with us, Saturday – about eight?'

Everybody, it appeared, would be pleased to 'pop across'. Baz asked shyly if he could bring Miss Denholm. Of course he could. She was now visiting him every weekend. They were in the best room of The Ship every Saturday night. They would sit, their heads quite close together, and talk quietly and smile at each other a lot. If they stood, Baz towered protectively over her and she lived warm and confident in the hollow of his body.

I wish I had the courage of the Victorian host who used to print on his invitations, 'Come at eight, go at eleven.'

The beer arrived on Friday afternoon, in three plastic casks, their bodies banded and grooved to simulate the staves and hoops of real casks. We set them on a trestle table, nailing laths alongside each one to stop them rolling, and covered them with white cloths. I fetched a pint glass from the kitchen and sampled the brew, holding the glass low to build up a head. It wasn't at all bad.

Saturday morning found me up at the crack of dawn. The dogs eyed me suspiciously as I crept barefoot about the kitchen. I had brought a butter-basketful of twigs into the kitchen to dry and, after blowing up the embers with the bellows, I set the twigs criss-cross in the grate. Grey-blue smoke curled lazily through the small structure and a flame licked enquiringly once or twice, before sharp fingers of flame rose with a hissing sound through the centre of the twigs. I layered coal and twigs on top of the fire until it was half-way up the chimney back and, calling the dogs, went out to see the stock.

I like Saturday mornings. I do not do any deliveries and leave the shop work to Vicky and, although nearly all the afternoons are taken up by a sale, I selfishly keep the mornings for myself. I do a little smallholding: a little hedging or ditching or mucking out and sometimes, if I am up early, I go and watch Ted milk – but this morning I had time for nothing. I hurried round the ducks and hens and pushed a complaining goat into the orchard.

The fire had drawn through and the tall stack of burning coals had settled into the grate. I piled on more coal and gave it several blasts with the bellows. With the draw tin clipped on to the bars the fire roared, and soon I could take it off carefully, for the brass knob was hot, and break the red-hot coals under the oven. I pushed oven sticks into the flue, took the inspection hatch off the side of the oven and watched the trembling spearheads of flame.

The meat flopped heavily on to my chest as I eased it off the bacon hooks. I washed it carefully, for small bits of lint from the muslin were stuck to it. The big tin was rinsed and smeared with fat. The meat filled it. I speared six cloves of garlic on to it, slid it into the oven and looked at the clock. A quarter to seven. Cooking in the coal-fired oven is not a precise process. If a wind gets up from the west the chimney draws better and the side of the oven will glow dull red. It is then that the pie-top is burnt and the stew crusts over. We like the oven. Meat is kept moist and bread rises to perfection. The oven is to work at; the little steel rake, its handle worn the colour of new pewter, is plied under the oven, coals are spread and pushed or raked out, and the damper clicked in and out on its toothed quadrant to keep an even heat. Thievin' Jack had insisted that we 'do it slow'.

There wasn't a sale that afternoon so I was going to have a selfish day – I had done my bit, the rest was women's and children's work. I heard Vicky's footsteps creak over the ceiling; she slopped down the stairs in my slippers and dressing gown and curled herself up in the Windsor chair, clutched her coffee and stared heavy-eyed into the fire. She is not a morning person.

Ted had finished milking and I helped him carry the full units down to the milk-house and pour them into the bulk tank.

White waves lapped against the stainless-steel sides, then subsided, and a covering of yellow cream rose and held the surface still. I had done a deal with Ted: I had sold myself into two days of slavery at haytime in return for a fallen ash tree for the fire.

Topic put her neck into the collar as we breasted the hill in the twenty-five-acre, and by the time we reached the fallen tree she was breathing heavily. She was getting too fat. All morning the angry buzz of the chainsaw deafened me and my wellingtons filled with chips as the pile of logs grew.

I was late back for lunch – it had taken longer to load the cart than I had anticipated – and Vicky tapped and beckoned at the kitchen window as I put on Topic's nosebag and sheeted her up.

The kitchen was warm and the smell of the cooking meat welled out into it when I opened the oven door. I still had the crushed spoon we had used for basting the goose and I just managed to get it down to the end of the tin, for the joint had not shrunk at all. The rind of fat, now honey-coloured, sizzled as I spooned the liquid fat over it. Vicky doesn't approve of garlic and had taken half the cloves off.

Peter and Sally sat at the table, absorbed in their work. They were skewering cubes of cheese and little flaps of boiled ham on to cocktail sticks and topping them off with olives. Sausages from the griddle were cut carefully into lengths, to suffer the same fate.

With the heat of the kitchen, and tired from a morning's logging, I was soon hard asleep.

233

Chapter 23

Fiery Frank's van awakened me as he reversed up to the orchard gate. Little Petal opened the back doors and threw out two canvas bags. They had brought a frame tent and she set to work joining the aluminium tubes together. Fiery carried his disco equipment through to the dining room. He hammered nails into my precious beam to hold his stroboscope lights and clustered the sockets with plugs. I heard the tap of one of the casks squeak on and the dribbling of beer into a mug. The microphone was tapped and blown at, and Fiery's voice boomed through the open door, 'Do not forsake me, oh my darling –'

Fiery helped me carry the trays of glasses over from The Ship and by seven o'clock we were ready. The joint had been lifted out on to the goose plate and the trays of snacks and stand pies waited under clean white cloths. The punch was sniffed and tested and several of the bobbing orange segments disappeared into mischievous little mouths. We put a card table alongside the fire, for the children were going to have a late supper. With Fiery in charge of the music it was going to be a noisy night, and the more tired they were when they climbed the stairs the more chance they would have of getting to sleep.

Vicky had changed into her best black dress and, although I did not have a suit, I felt quite smart in my new moleskin trousers and blue sweater. Little Petal had got the tent up and was now sitting by the side of the fireplace. The girl likes eating; she had got a big piece of stand pie and her upper lip stretched over the lower as she tried to retrieve a piece of jellied gravy. Fiery had put on a Beatles tape and was teaching Sally to jive. She was nearly as tall as the little man and went through the movements self-consciously, while he was a fluid, easy mover. Peter had been sneaking some punch. I could tell because the peppering of nutmeg was swirling over the top of the big bowl and the glass he had dipped in had left a half-moon stain on the cloth. I smiled at him and he grinned back, relieved. I lit both fires, got Peter to help me bring in logs and set a pile by each fireplace. Vicky was worried about the punch – was it too strong? We had bottles of fruit juices for the non-drinkers.

People arrived in clumps. There was me, Vicky and the children, Little Petal and Frank and then the clump bringing Mr and Mrs Lewis, old Mr Hall, Nellie May and Rabbit arrived. I honed the big carving knife on the back window sill and started carving the meat. Vicky served the punch and Fiery, whistling merrily, broke off the jiving lessons and filled glasses from the beer casks. He soon had Rabbit Joe laughing.

'Just let me know when that's empty, old lad. There's plenty more where that's come from.'

Nellie May refused the punch and settled herself alongside Little Petal with a pint of beer.

Canary Mary had sent a message with Long John – she had jaundice and could not come.

The next clump brought Baz and Miss Denholm, the Radfords, Thievin' Jack and Ivy and Miss Wells. By half past eight both the lounge and the dining room were full of people. Colin Vernon arrived with a tarty bird and Billy Potts followed them up the hallway, unable to take his eyes off Tarty Bird's wiggling bottom. With such an audience, Fiery could resist it no longer; he drew two pints and leaped on to his makeshift stage. With his eyes closed and the microphone hidden in cupped hands, his trembling voice vibrated across the room, 'Do not forsake me . . .'

Billy Potts crammed a piece of stand pie into each waistcoat pocket, thrust out a none-too-clean hand and took a piece of meat as it curled from my knife.

Little Petal and Nellie May had common ground: both read the cards and had an interest in the occult. They put their heads together and ignored Rabbit, who sat on a milking stool at their feet listening intently to every word. When they had emptied their glasses they handed them silently to Rabbit, who hurried to the table and refilled them quickly. He didn't want to miss anything.

Colin and Tarty Bird were dancing slowly, cheek to cheek. Mr and Mrs Lewis and old Mr Hall watched them silently. Tarty Bird had a black leather mini skirt, fully fashioned black stockings and shoes so high-heeled she could hardly walk in them. Mrs Lewis disapproved; both men shyly smiled their approval. Fiery discovered that the tiny shelf to the right of the fireplace would just hold two pint glasses. He broke off right in the middle of 'Do not forsake me' and jumped from his little stage to refill his two glasses. The Beatles dutifully took over and the dancers quickened.

Vicky was busy dispensing the punch. I had carved half the

joint and slit each slice in two, rolling them unevenly and setting them around the plate. The meat was pink in the middle and evenly grained. Ted made little packets of his slices and filled them with chopped onion. With enough of the meat cut, I turned my head to bar keeping. I was not good at it; filling two glasses at a time, I either got too much head or none at all. The pool of spilt beer grew and was trodden across the room. The children were still up, weaving through the crowd with their small trays of offerings, and I mentioned to Vicky that it was time they were in bed. Their faces wrinkled up in disgust as they were steered into the kitchen for supper. I had built up the fires unnecessarily for it was quite warm in both rooms, and on my way back to the beer table the Colonel seized my arm.

'Who is that fellow?' He nodded towards Fiery who was back on the stage, nestling two new pints on to the shelf.

'Ah! He's a Lancastrian, Colonel.'

The grey head nodded knowingly and he raised his eyes to the ceiling, before making off to buttonhole the vicar.

Billy Potts was watching Fiery, a constant grin split his brick-red face; he had never come across anybody like him.

Long John fetched a pint for old Mr Hall and laced it liberally with Swaledale Lightning. The old man's eyes were sparkling; he tapped a horny hand on his knee to the music and ignored his daughter's chastening stare.

The punch was getting low and Vicky emptied our last bottle of spirits into it. She swilled it around with the ladle, washing the moustache of grated nutmeg from the side of the bowl. The shortage of punch made me look at the beer casks; by rocking them from side to side I judged they were about half full. It was nine o'clock. Fiery jumped from the stage with his empty glasses. Billy nodded at them.

'Tha wants a bucket, lad.' Fiery raised a forefinger to his brow and disappeared into the shop. He returned with a Victorian chamber pot and, after wiping the inside carefully, he filled it to the brim with beer. This made Billy laugh until his top set was completely dislodged.

We had the first casualty of the night. Old Mr Hall passed out and was carried into the garden, where the cold night air soon brought him round. Mrs Lewis bullied him home. 'Silly old sod, nearly eighty an' showing us up like that.' He looked awful; beads of sweat stood out on his bald head, he breathed deeply and leaned heavily on his daughter's arm. The path back to the shop shimmered in the moonlight, his head held a cacophony of ringing and jangling and there was an awful creeping nausea which kept rising from his stomach to make him gasp and blow, but he was happy. Tarty Bird had sat on his knee for a good five minutes.

The punch bowl was completely empty. Vicky had abandoned it to dance with Colin, and Rabbit stood in front of it with Little Petal's empty glass. Ivy stood behind him with her empty glass and behind her were two women I had never seen before. I grabbed the bowl and hurried into the kitchen. A frantic search produced a bottle of cooking sherry and three fingers of gin. I splashed these into the bowl and grated nutmeg over it. It looked pathetic. There were twelve bottles of Swaledale Lightning on the dairy shelf – a little would fill out the bowl and make it presentable.

Long John had been lacing everybody's beer with it for the last hour to no ill effect, so I poured in three bottles and gave it a stir. I watched Ivy carefully as she took her first sip. She showed no adverse reaction so I made a quick decision. Nipping into the dairy I grabbed two more bottles. They

238

carried labels of a famous gin and Dolly smiled appreciatively as they glugged into the bowl.

Both rooms were hot and smoky and the noise was deafening. Baz and Miss Denholm slipped out of the back door as the taproom gang came in the front, red beaming faces, for they had not been idle.

Billy cornered them excitedly. 'Yon little fella, he's supping out of a pittle pot.' Fiery raised the chamber pot in salute and the gang started to fill glasses from the casks. Long John fetched several more bottles from his van and laced each pint.

At ten o'clock Charlie closed The Ship and walked, bottle in hand, across the green. 'Nothing kills trade like some silly bugger giving it away.'

Vicky was dancing with Thievin' Jack; he was making her laugh. She threw her head back and the light from Fiery's strobes sent cascades of colour down her gorgeous hair. Ted palmed Dolly on to the Colonel and went and sat with Ivy. He had always fancied her. She stretched out her legs and giggled like a schoolgirl as he whispered in her ear, 'I only married her for her gravy.'

In the other room, Colin was chatting up the Martins's attractive daughter. She is horse-mad, so Colin boasted of his prowess in the hunting field. His stories were painfully transparent, but the girl was too polite to question them.

The Radfords had to leave early, for their babysitter is only young and Richard had to have her home for eleven. The vicar was a little unsteady as he searched the village green for his beloved Morris. He sat in it for half an hour with the windows wound down before he turned the key and drove slowly home, hoping Stephanie was in bed.

The taproom boys stood around the table. Beer had

sharpened their appetites and soon all the stand pies and slices of meat had disappeared. The underkeeper was standing in front of the fire, the room was oppressively hot but he didn't seem to notice the heat. He was wearing a heavy tweed suit and a turtle-neck sweater. He cradled a pint of beer to his chest as his free hand searched through his pockets.

Fiery was intuitive: he realized the Colonel did not like him and was determined to change this. He came half-way up the Colonel's waistcoat, so his head was held well back as he smiled up at him.

'Well, Colonel, what regiment?'

I was surprised. I expected 'guv' or 'General', but Fiery knows how people tick. The Colonel is ex-Indian Army.

Fiery gave him his impressed look. 'Both me and me dad was Lancashire Fusiliers. Indian Division took some stick in the first one, didn't they?'

The Colonel smiled.

Ivy had just slapped Ted's face when the thick underkeeper, rocking slightly on his feet, threw a fistful of old raffle tickets on the fire. Nestling among them were several two-two bullets. Two rapid explosions sent a shower of sparks bursting from the fireplace and a piece of lead zinging across the room to embed itself in the beam. A column of soot dropped down the chimney and, striking the hearth, billowed out into the room.

Colin dived under the table, several women started to scream and Billy, coughing violently, lurched to the door, his left wellington caught in the tangle of wires Fiery had spliced into the double socket. The room was plunged into darkness.

The coughing and spluttering guests poured out on to the village green, a cloud of soot drifting after them.

Vicky raced upstairs to see that the children were all right as I took the cover off the fuse box and fumbled with the thin wire. The soot cloud subsided quickly. Ted opened the windows and, as soon as the lights flicked on again, people started to traipse back in. The heavy soot smell caused them to wrinkle their noses and a few to sneeze, but they dusted off the seats and soon everything was back to normal.

Near the fireplace, a thick layer of soot covered everything. The punch bowl was a disc of black and my beloved joint, my superb haunch of bull beef, was black; it sat on its black oval plate like a crouching vulture.

The water swirled down the drain like black ink as I rotated the joint under the tap. I estimated that there was at least twenty pounds' worth left as I carefully scrubbed into the tiny crevices with a nail brush.

In the dining room, Dolly's charring instinct overcame her concern for her new dress as she skimmed the soot off the punch, gingerly folded the cloths on the beer casks and, with slow, deliberate strokes of a hand brush, returned the invading soot to the fireplace.

Fiery did not bother to plug his music machine back in. He and the Colonel were sitting, black-faced, on the little stage, singing 'The Road to Mandalay'.

The taproom gang, always loath to leave free alcohol, pulled their stools around in a circle and set the punch bowl in the middle.

Ivy had left Thievin' Jack on the lounge floor; she had taken his keys out of his pocket and growled home up the dale in the travelling shop. She couldn't get it out of second gear and complained bitterly of the play in the steering.

Billy was still under the table. There had been intermittent snatches of song, 'I'm Billy Potts of Altonshotts . . .', but he had been quiet for the last hour.

Vicky was leaning her head against the door jamb, her eyes closed. I packed her off to bed and helped Ted to lift Rabbit off the floor and on to a stool. He was out to the world. Little Petal took Nellie May home and was coming back up the yard when the underkeeper lurched up to her and put his arms around her ample waist.

'Give us a kiss, luv.'

Little Petal's face was expressionless. She brought her left knee up into his groin and the underkeeper gasped in pain, buckled and fell sideways into the Dutch barn. She slopped on into the house and picked up the singing Fiery. She cradled him in her fat arms, his head pressed against her ample bosom.

The Colonel was very drunk; his hairpiece had been pushed to one side revealing a crescent of pink scalp, there were several sooty fingerprints where he had groped absentmindedly, half aware that something was amiss. He staggered through the kitchen after Little Petal, dislodging several prints and the spoon rack as he banged against the wall.

'Be careful with that little fella there – he's NCO material.'

At two o'clock in the morning there were just two of the tap-room gang left. They were sitting on the floor with their backs against the wall, and the one who had lost a boot had the empty punch bowl on his head.

Ted backed his tractor up to the front door and we lifted Rabbit, Thievin' Jack and the underkeeper into the link box. With a little coaxing, the rear guard of the taproom gang reluc-tantly parted with the punch bowl and tottered out to drop on to the link box. Ted started the engine and jolted across the green with his joggling load of bodies. I didn't know where he was taking them and I didn't care.

I had never been so tired in my life. I was half-way up the stairs when I remembered Billy Potts, still under the table. He had no scruples when it came to food or alcohol, so I lurched back down to the kitchen, took the wet joint off the draining board, wrapped it in a towel and took it to bed with me.

Vicky was still asleep. She slept like a young child, with her knees drawn up and her hands openly clasped under her chin. Her blonde hair was spread over the pillow and strands of it fell softly over her face. I shook her shoulder and she turned, half on her back. The hands disappeared slowly under the clothes and she swallowed two or three times, making soft sucking noises before she opened her eyes and smiled up at me.

The coffee was hot. I took mine to the window and looked out at the village green. It was still very early: over the tops of the houses the fells were hung with a grey mist and only a bright band of lighter grey washed at its upper edge, with the palest of yellows showing where the sky began. 'The most beautiful cat in the world' walked gingerly on top of the Lewises' railings. The Colonel's Maran cockerel crowed – a confident, challenging, 'throw off your fetters' crow.

Ted's little grey Ferguson whined on the starter; blue puffs burst from the exhaust as it coughed and failed to catch. I couldn't hear Ted, but I knew he would be cursing, 'Bloody pig – allus been a bad starter.' He kicked the tyre and I just caught sight of his head as he went back into the milk-house and fetched the Easy-Start. Next time the engine caught, he revved it fiercely and the brakes squealed as the little tractor jolted out of the farmyard and passed under the window.

I waved, raising the coffee cup to eye level. Ted saw me, his head thrust against the milky perspex panels of the cab like a huge fish bumping the glass in an aquarium. He gave me a thumbs-up and sped off down the village, a blue plume rising from the rocking tractor.

I heard Vicky yawn and stretch. The bed springs creaked as she leaned out and dumped the empty cup on the bedside table. She yawned again and buried her head in the pillow. The half-eaten joint was still on the dressing table; the delicate little crocheted doilies were trapped, crumpled and folded, under the edge of the huge plate.

I could hardly hear Vicky. 'Did it go all right?'

Mrs Lewis, refreshed by a night's sleep, renewed her verbal attack on her father. In the tent, Little Petal's fat arms cradled Fiery and the Colonel like two sucking babes while the goat chewed the Colonel's expensive hairpiece. Down in the five-acre barn the link box full of casualties stretched and yawned in the straw. Ivy banged the kettle under the tap and wondered how she was going to explain to Thievin' Jack why his precious van was half submerged in Tinker's Pond. Long John stirred slowly into life under a pile of army greatcoats, and told himself that he didn't at all mind waking up with a thick head – the day can only get better. In a lay-by somewhere on the A19, Colin blinked at the dawn and vaguely wondered what had happened to Tarty Bird. Miss Denholm stood barefoot on Baz's kitchen floor. A blanket pulled around her, she forked rashers of bacon into a pan with the handle of her comb. Billy Potts had just loaded half a dozen bullocks and was delighted to find a piece of stand pie in his waistcoat pocket.

I pressed my aching forehead against the cold windowpane. 'Yes, my love, I think it went all right.'

244

Coming soon from Sphere, more

Tales from the Dales

THE LUCK OF A COUNTRYMAN

September 2011

The enchanting sequel to *A Countryman's Lot*, which told the story of Max Hardcastle's move to the Yorkshire Dales and the richness of life as an antiques dealer, *The Luck of a Countryman* contains an array of eccentric characters and curious situations which are guaranteed to delight and amuse. Old favourites reappear in new – and sometimes alarming – situations. And a myriad of new personalities join in the ups and downs of life in the Dales.

Life is not all plain sailing, but the Hardcastles join in wholeheartedly with the trials and triumphs that beset the peaceful village of Ramsthwaite. How will they ever shift Thievin' Jack's van from the pond? And will the wedding of the year go off smoothly?

THE COUNTRY BUSINESS

March 2012

In this third volume of tales from the Dales, the
Hardcastle family continue their life among the colourful
inhabitants of Ramsthwaite. Whilst village characters, such
as Canary Mary and Fiery Frank, divert them with a variety
of bizarre adventures, Max and Vicky are still facing
challenges on their smallholding. Their antiques business, on
the other hand, is thriving, and attracts as many curios as
ever, such as crystal balls, a station clock and a locked safe.
As the year proceeds towards the annual Hound Trail, the
village enjoys its customary ups and downs – events
brought beautifully to life by Max Hardcastle in this
warmly engaging memoir.